The Guided Heart

Moving Through Grief and Finding Spiritual Solace

Victoria L. Volk

Print ISBN: 978-0-9992434-0-4

Cover Art by Jenny Ambrose

Cover photo by © Kimberly C. Roberts

Typesetting by Polgarus Studio

Dedication

For my dad, Willard Richard Becker—a Vietnam veteran, husband of 17 years, father of three, and stepfather to one, for whom I write this book in memoriam. In your life and beyond your death, you have taught me how to find gratitude, empathy, and compassion. Forgive me for dwelling on the date of your death, for it is the only date I have ever remembered. I hope I've made you proud.

For Tony, the encourager of my dreams and the keeper of my heart, and our children, Xavier, Alexandra, and Jozlyn. Each of you have grown and stretched me in so many ways and are a daily reminder to be present in the moment.

Contents

Foreword

Victoria and I met at a period in our lives when we had both spent a lot of time and energy on our personal growth and spiritual development. We were both, in our own way, trying to surmount that last "hurdle" to overcome the grief and abuse we had experienced in our lives. We were also both searching for the "true" us, and working towards getting back to the happy contentment most would associate with our youth, and that which would allow us to fully embrace life. I was in the role of a life coach, and Victoria was my client, however through our soulful relationship, we both accelerated our personal and spiritual growth together, as often happens with connections we make in life.

When I read this book, I was in awe of Victoria's deep self-awareness, courageousness, and wisdom. The ego part of me was proud of her growth, and I felt a deep sense of satisfaction for the part I played in helping her on her journey. My soul sang with joy seeing my soul sister come full circle in her evolution and growth.

To this day, I am not sure Victoria knows just how much she contributed to my growth as well. You see, when we are grieving, and growing through our spiritual journey, we can feel all alone in the world. The truth is that grief unites us, as it is something we all face in our lives. In spiritual truth we are never alone, and remembering this can bring us comfort and hope.

Grief can allow us to understand and expand our perspective, and help us to deepen our connection with others. It can also remind us that we are all unified with a desire to be happy, express love, and experience joy in our lives. Knowing these truths, we can choose to switch our perspective to an acknowledgement and validation of this inevitable human experience. This acceptance can lead to us allowing ourselves, as we would our brothers and sisters, to really feel, and release the deep emotions that come with a significant loss, or major change in our lives.

If we do not resist these very human emotions, and embrace a faith in a higher purpose, we can open up to the blessings and lessons that come from these pivotal times in our lives. In time, this awareness, acceptance, and faith can foster profound gratitude in our lives:

⇒ Gratitude for the growth, lessons, and increased strength we gain from the experience;
⇒ Gratitude for the memories, and love we hold in our hearts;
⇒ Gratitude for the possibilities and opportunities these experiences bring into our lives; and
⇒ Gratitude for the contrast grief allows for us to appreciate the beauty and wonders that life has to offer.

You see, without these varied human experiences, we could not fully appreciate the many beautiful, loving, and joyful moments of our lives, and the people with whom we share these blessings every day.

Imagine for a moment what life would be like if there was no awareness of our finite experience on this planet, and the inevitability of an end to our human existence on the earth. Without the "low points" we have nothing with which to compare the beautiful wonders of the world, and we could not have the same appreciation for the many joys in life.

Would we cherish our loved ones the same?

Would we use the gift of our free will to follow our dreams?

I dare say we would not, for we would have no point of reference to fully embrace every precious moment of our lives, INCLUDING those that give us no choice but to look at death and loss, and consequently give us the opportunity to embrace all of our human existence…roses, thorns and all!

Victoria lovingly shares the importance of:

- ⇒ Commitment and consistency to our healing…no matter how long it takes!
- ⇒ Sharing our experiences with others so that we don't feel alone, and helping each other through what has worked for us;
- ⇒ Exploring what our trials and tribulations teach us about ourselves and others;
- ⇒ The power of choosing to allow ourselves to do what we love, and be happy, no matter what!
- ⇒ Taking care of YOU so that you can take care of others; and, most importantly;
- ⇒ Remembering that we are all unique, but that both our grief, and our desire to be at peace, binds us all as one!

Enjoy the inspiration and tools that Victoria courageously shares, and remember just how much you are loved and cherished!

Peace and Blessings,

Angela

Introduction

"*Put yourself in the way of beauty.*"

- The mother of author Cheryl Strayed

There is a tendency to run when life gets hard and challenging. There is also a tendency to blame anyone but ourselves when things go awry. Like many, I have experienced a multitude of childhood trauma. In addition to the loss of my father, I also experienced several incidences of molestation by a friend of the family, and in early adulthood, the loss of my stepfather to divorce and later death. Despite him being away for work more often than he was home, he was the only father figure I had all of my teen years.

Naive in the ways of the world and still trying to find my way, further into young adulthood, I would experience the loss of a first romantic relationship, as well as a dear woman I cared for in Hospice Home Health. Like a lot of people, I also endured the loss of friendships, numerous personal failures, and likely more, if I gave it more thought.

I know loss like the back of my hand: loss of love, support, emotional guidance, my innocence, confidence, self-worth, etc. I also know beauty: in the human spirit, in nature, and in pain. The quote used in this introduction was shared by the author of *Wild*, Cheryl Strayed, in an interview. As I watched this interview, I could have said the very words she shared, as every word she said resonated with me. I haven't even read her book, but I know I will now, as it describes her personal journey with grief after losing her mother. It's fitting, because after all the grief I've endured, I've grown to be drawn to others grief experiences.

In the interview, Strayed went on to share the lessons her mother passed on to her. When life didn't go the way she thought it should, her mother would remind her *it's on you; life is hard, but you don't have to stay in that feeling.* Instead, she told her "put yourself in the way of beauty." Strayed went on to explain what her mother meant: there will always be a sunrise and sunset—you choose if you will be there or not.

I relate to this. Unlike Strayed, I didn't have a person in my life to say such words to me. Yes, I had support when I needed it from a few trusted souls, but no one ever gave me a kick in the pants. No one told me the hard stuff I needed to hear. Instead, it was a long, windy road for me to figure it all out for myself, taking decades to unravel the weave of emotion and personal baggage.

I simply do not want this for you. This book is my personal journey with grief and emotional pain, and the lessons I've gleaned from my life experience. Yours will be different, yes, but my hope is that something within these pages resonates with you, just as I found comfort in other people's stories of grief and emotional pain.

The question I think all of us who have experienced emotional pain ask is: how do we endure our suffering? We all work through it in different ways. In the following pages, I dive more deeply into how I endured my own. I hope this book gives you the courage to dive into your suffering, so you too can let it go and move on. You will never forget, this I know, but if you can embrace the lessons that suffering teaches us, it will change your personal grief story—and your future.

Life is hard, challenging, messy, and far from a straight line. But there is beauty along the way, moving parallel with us as we travel through each day. I only wish I had stopped to appreciate all the beauty this life had to offer long ago—to feel it, and believe that emotional pain only lasts as long as we allow it to.

My message is this: it is never too late to start again. And again. And again, if you need to. Begin by questioning your thoughts. Slowly, you'll peel away the layers. Only then can the real inner work begin.

I have a suggestion before you turn the page and dive into the chapters that follow. Silently to yourself, or better yet, on paper, answer the following questions, or, at the very least, keep them in the back of your mind:

- What do I want to experience in life?
- How do I want to grow?
- What do I want to contribute to the planet?

I neither hold a PhD, nor do I have scientific data to fall back on for the points made in this book. What I do have is an intimate experience with grief that spans the majority of my life. That said, I don't feel my story is any more special than your own. Because, as I'll allude to over and over throughout these pages, we all have a story. I share mine, finally, after two years of having this deep desire to share a message of hope for those who may have had a similar experience. Also, I share for those who are seeking a different perspective on grief, perhaps to make more sense of their own, which I hope this book can do for you.

This book is not a how-to guide book from a licensed therapist. What is held within these pages is a vulnerability I've only ever truly been able to express in the written word, which has helped me more than anything else in my life. My hope is that these words leave you with a feeling of hope and inspire that deep desire within you that I know you have, to fully live life again out from behind the shadow of your sorrow.

I will close this introduction with more words from Cheryl Strayed, as I couldn't have said it better myself:

"Nobody's going to do your life for you. You have to do it yourself, whether you're rich or poor, out of money or raking it in, the beneficiary of ridiculous fortune or terrible injustice. And you have to do it no matter what is true. No matter what is hard. No matter what unjust, sad, or sucky things have befallen you. Self-pity is a dead-end road. You make a choice to drive down it. It's up to you to decide to stay parked there or turn around and drive out."

Let's start driving out, shall we? Embrace the hard self-work. Trust me; it's a lot easier than being emotionally trapped day after day and living life on autopilot. Let's do this—and if you get stuck along the way, reach out to me; you are never alone.

PART I:

We All Have a Story

1

What Is Your Grief Story?

*"Life is not a matter of holding good cards,
but of playing a poor hand well."*

- Robert Louis Stevenson

"She doesn't understand anyway," I heard someone say, talking about me as if I wasn't even there.

March 31st, 1987 is the anniversary of my father's death. On July 30th of that year, he would have turned forty-five years old. He spent the last two years of his life (after having been given only six months to live) fighting a battle he knew he wouldn't win. The doctors said there was nothing they could do; the cancer had spread to surrounding tissue and organs.

Colon cancer took my father away, and my mother became a widow at forty-three years old, being left to raise two children still living at home—myself (age eight) and my brother (fourteen at the time). I'm not sure any woman in her position, or any woman who has been in her position,

9

would know what to do, how to do it, or how to navigate raising grieving children while grieving themselves.

It was impossible for me to understand then the profound effect my father's death would have on me. By the time I was ten years old, I would begin to grasp exactly that.

Two years after the death of my father, my mother remarried. The new man in her life was a long-haul truck driver and was home, typically, every other weekend. Theirs was a tumultuous relationship. There were many disputes during their nine-year marriage, and it ultimately ended in divorce. I learned during that time, and from the time of my father's death, that my mother was emotionally incapable of being there for both my brother and myself. I grew up quickly, as did my brother.

I wasn't a child who lashed out or got into mischief. Rather, I was the wallflower, the introvert, the shy girl in the corner who spoke up when spoken to. And honestly, to this day, I'm not quite sure how I managed my grief as a young girl (particularly in elementary school) other than stuffing it all down.

My mother did not know what to do for my brother or myself. There was no grief counseling, and for reasons still unclear to this day, my father's family ceased to exist in my life following the funeral. So, from a young age, my family was my immediate family, as well as some family on my mother's side—quite small in comparison to what I would later marry into in adulthood.

Learning to Cope

It wasn't until journaling was a requirement for English class in high school that I started to express my feelings. I wrote poetry, started journaling for myself (in addition to journaling for class), and for the first time, I began to feel some of what I stuffed down for so many years.

During this period in my life, there were several occasions where I lashed out at my mother, often out of frustration that had built up within me over the years. I don't know if my mother knew *how* to be there for me; she couldn't emotionally care for herself. I detached myself as much as I could. Being a teenager is hard enough, but being a female teenager of an emotionally trapped mother is even harder. Therefore, we never developed a mother-daughter bond that I would have loved to have shared with her. I think she realized the daughter who had taken emotional care of her all those years was eventually leaving, too.

My childhood is where my grief story began; however, it's certainly not where it ended. There would be several more lessons to follow in my life. I believe there are different "faces" grief presents during our lives. And often, it presents itself in ways you'd least expect.

The "Faces" of Grief

On some level, I still grieve for the "normal" childhood I could have had, had my father's untimely death not happened. But in reality, I'll never know what that "other" life would have been. So, it's the not knowing, not getting the chance, that I would come to deal with years later as well. I grieve for all the moments in my life my dad was never a part of: protecting me as fathers do, walking me down the aisle, seeing and knowing his grandchildren and likewise, my children knowing their grandfather. These are the things I still grieve for. Grief, in my opinion, never leaves. It is not something to *get over*. It is something to sit with, work through, and live with—just in a different way as the years go on.

At some point in life, all of us experience grief. Whether it be losing someone we love, a divorce, devastating financial loss, loss of career, even infertility—all cause some form of emotional pain. How we cope with it can mean months, or even years, maybe even decades of loss of well-being. That, to me, is tragic. When we remain emotionally paralyzed, we do ourselves, those still in our lives, our communities, and our world, a disservice.

Through my life, I can pinpoint at least nine pain points where I experienced a feeling of loss. Many have to do with death due to illness; however, not all. I have grieved lost opportunity (not knowing my father's family or having a relationship with them), lost time with my kids because, in my previous business, I was so driven to prove something, as well as loss of friendships and relationships.

No matter how grief appears in your life, it's sure to make you feel as though you're no longer in control. You may become aware of your own mortality, which itself can cause self-reflection. When we self-reflect, we often realize our shortcomings or focus on the negative. It is being faced with uncomfortable feelings that arise from grief that shake us. Often, we just don't know what to do with those feelings. At least, I know my mother didn't. As a result, neither did I—and so, this dynamic played out for decades.

Your Grief Story

What is your grief story? If you haven't experienced the loss of a loved one, which I presume is why you picked up this book and decided to turn its pages, but rather experienced the loss of love, career, or even health—these are still losses that cause some level of grief.

Have you ever considered all that has been handed your way in life that has caused you emotional pain in some way? What are those moments that have stuck with you, which have given you a lingering feeling of loss? Maybe it wasn't what was but what could have been?

I don't think there is a person out there who hasn't experienced any form of grief. As a parent myself, I cannot even fathom the helplessness and hopelessness my dad must've felt, and the thoughts that ran through his mind when he received his diagnosis. To know that you won't be around to watch your children grow, that you will never see your grandchildren, or witness your kids get married. All of the hopes and dreams of living a full life with your spouse are shattered in one sentence spoken by a doctor sitting across from you in a sterile, impersonal office.

It's easy to think of *my* grief, but it deepens my sadness when I acknowledge what my father must have experienced. Sometimes, just trying to place ourselves in the shoes of another changes our perspective. In my case, I am humbled when I think of the strength my father showed all of us; the fight within him, to hang on for just one more day, month, and ultimately two more years.

My grief consumed me for many years. I will touch on certain aspects of what I mean as the chapters progress. For now, the first three chapters will focus on grief itself; from a spiritual perspective, the ways it can present itself in our lives, and a preface on getting it resolved.

A Spiritual Journey with Grief

I think it is important I make it abundantly clear that I am coming from a spiritual place in my heart. I do not wish to stuff my beliefs down your throat, as much as I don't want judgment passed for feeling the way I do. All of us have a unique spiritual path we follow. Mine has certainly been full of twists and turns.

Before my father's passing, we were a typical Lutheran family, attending church every Sunday, as well as Sunday school. After my dad's death, however, all of that changed. We stopped going to church altogether. I did attend confirmation classes and was confirmed Lutheran. However, it would either have to be a funeral or wedding for me to set foot in a church of any kind until I was twenty-three, when my husband and I began our relationship.

I was bitter for many years. Granted, I had a lot of years to be bitter. Fortunately, life worked out for me the way it did, as I prayed, received, and really, it's as simple as that. After many years of not having the ability to pray from the heart, life had finally handed me more grief than I could bear. Feeling tapped out emotionally, and overwhelmed, I prayed because I simply did not know what else to do. The rest is history, so to speak. Everything changed moving forward.

Before my husband came into my life as more than a friend, I was on a self-destructive path. I was becoming an expert at goodbyes and led a very narcissistic lifestyle. I don't know what my husband saw in me, honestly. At that point we had known each other for seven years, since we met in high school. But he was a far better human being then than I was—bar none.

It was one more experience with grief when I was twenty-one that was, in simple terms, the straw that broke the camel's back. A five-year relationship was over, as was the life I thought we were going to have. Later, this loss would prove to be a blessing in disguise—which, as my life illustrates, can be the case at times. Surely, when it comes to relationships, you may relate as well.

Sometimes we just don't understand what it is that is best for us. Our minds tell us one thing, while our hearts and intuition tell us another, and we tend to choose the path of least resistance (and pain). It's also difficult to discern the best decision when you are caught up in emotion. We tend to check rationality at the door when we have a grandiose view of ourselves, the world, and those we perch up on pedestals. My self-worth was non-existent. Thankfully, God showed me a better way.

More on my spiritual journey with grief in detail in Chapter 3—in the meantime, know that for me, a higher power seemed like a very out-of-reach concept for me. Acknowledgment: of all that had gone wrong and all that had gone right, this was the first baby step on my journey to resolving my grief.

Steps Towards Resolving Grief

As I've previously mentioned, grief has many "faces." I touched on a few ways I've experienced different forms of it myself. For instance, closing my photography business after six years was one of the most difficult decisions I have made. I know how much of myself I poured into creating and maintaining my business all those years. The time, money, sweat equity, not to mention the sleep deprivation while raising three young children (ages four and under at the time). It certainly was a labor of love.

I grieved for months leading up to my decision, as I knew it was what needed to be done at that stage in my life. I continued to wallow in my sadness until I finally decided to make it official with the selling of most of my gear over a year later. I found the act of officially letting go the hardest part.

Isn't that what grief ultimately causes us to do—let go of what was and what will never be again? Isn't that, too, what grief itself is—the emotional reaction to loss or change of any kind? We fight to hold on, and we fight to let go. That is the dilemma of grief, isn't it?

What I would like you to do is think of a moment in your life that caused you to have an emotional reaction to loss or a change of any kind. Close this book and reflect on the feelings that arise when your mind takes you back to a time such as this in *your* life. Go ahead—then open these pages again when ready.

Now, if you want to feel more strongly the impact that loss or change had on you, grab a notebook, a writing utensil, and head to a quiet space, or do this exercise as soon as it is convenient. Set a timer for thirty minutes and just write. If you're stumped on where to begin, finish this sentence: "The loss of _____ made me feel as though _____."

One thing to consider before doing this is to understand my intention, which is having you write out (possibly for the first time) your feelings surrounding the event that has shaken you to your core. When we release our feelings on paper, and I speak from personal experience, they tend to have less power over us, especially if we're in a place of not knowing who we can truly talk to. The act of writing our fears, worries, and emotional pain forces us to sit with those feelings and can be very therapeutic. I wholeheartedly believe that writing for our personal well-being is the cheapest therapy one can find, but I know few, even in my own life, who practice this.

How did that feel? Pretty raw, I imagine. It's painful to reflect on our pains, I get that. Truly, this is an exercise in acknowledgment. Taking inventory of the emotional baggage weighing us down day in and day out gives us a clearer picture of where we are emotionally right now. This inevitably aids you in figuring out where you would rather be.

2

Labeling Grief

"The quieter you become, the more you can hear."

- Baba Ram Dass

In the previous chapter, I brought up the idea that there may be a story of grief within you that you may not have even considered being a source of emotional pain. I hope the exercise, if completed, offered some clarity.

Amazing revelations can arise from sitting with our feelings and expressing them in some way. I realize every person is different and what works for one may not work for another. On the other hand, if it does offer a benefit, then I hope it is a practice that you will continue—either in the form of regular journaling or for those times where life is confusing and overwhelming.

Finding meaning to grief is another step in the process of becoming emotionally transparent when it comes to feelings of grief and loss, or, in some cases, drastic change that causes emotional turbulence.

When written out, feelings are metaphorically stamped with a label. Articulated emotion, written from thought with a pen to paper, gets it out of our heads and labels it just as it is. Like the death of my father, for example. The action of writing out that experience gives a subconscious label to my feelings: grief. I'm acknowledging my own feelings, labeling those feelings on a subconscious level, and at the same time *feeling* them.

Years later, I labeled my feelings as "longing." Because ultimately, I longed for a life I never got to have; a life the rest of my peers got to experience. As I grew, it was this feeling of "not having" and comparing what I didn't have to what everyone else around me did. Furthermore, it manifested in my life in various ways.

In my childhood, for example, on grandparents' day, everyone else had a grandparent present—except for me. I even have a photo to show a glimpse of this aspect of my life.

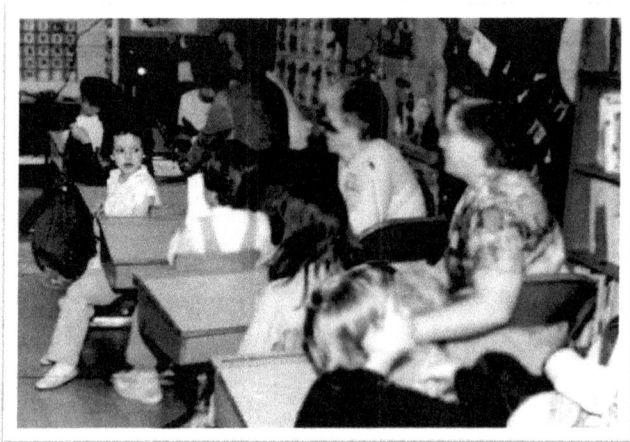

Just the fact that this is documented in a photograph makes me curious as to who took it and their reason for taking it. Was the one who took it taking pity on me? It really is quite a sad memento for me, one that reminds me that the very pains of my childhood may have left scars, but I am the person I am today because of those scars. Unfortunately, it would take me many years to feel stronger because of life's challenges, as opposed to taking on the role of "victim."

More on this in part two.

Fast-forward years later, into adulthood, and money became a huge block for me because I was making decisions from a place of lack due to having little self-worth and confidence. I was someone who, because I lacked self-worth, threw money at unnecessary things that, in the short term, would make me feel better. I think we all know that things don't equate to happiness. Look around, however, and you will see that emptiness and materialistic happiness are abundant, unfortunately.

Label the Grief

For now, I want to dive a bit more into the idea of labeling grief. Television personality and author Dr. Phil McGraw says, "You can't change what you don't acknowledge." I completely agree. What I mean when I say "labeling grief" is that by giving the feelings surrounding your grief a label is essentially calling those feelings what they are. I used my experience of grandparents' day as an example, although it's just a sliver of the bigger picture of emotion I experienced during that time.

Every notch etched on the proverbial emotional turbulence pole is another opportunity to fully experience, express, label, and eventually, let go. It's the ride of the emotional tide that caused me the most angst, and this is what keeps many of us who are experiencing grief, in whatever form, emotionally stuck and not going with the flow of life.

There is no "one size fits all" when it comes to how we acknowledge, express, define, and hopefully learn to cope with grief in a heart-centered way. Each of us who grieve, at any given point in our lives, must face the unknown, which is different for each and every one of us. No two circumstances are the same. My expression in these pages is based on my personal experience and perspective, having made it to the "lighter side" of grief. And by "lighter side," I mean that I am no longer bound by the emotional shackles of the past. My hope is that you, too, find your way to the "lighter side."

The Power of a Song

One of the things I remember doing as a teenager was walking nearly a mile in the dead of winter to the ice skating rink across town. I would carry my ice skates, which I received one year for Christmas (and still have to this day), and have my Walkman (80's kids will know just what I'm talking about) with my premixed cassette tapes filled with my favorite music of that time: Indigo Girls, Pearl Jam, and Dinosaur Jr. to name a few. I would sit in the snow to change from my snow boots to ice skates, as there was no warming house. I'd spend hours skating to the music, getting lost in the moment. It felt as though I was someone else and the world around me, along with my worries, seemingly melted away.

Life at home was far from an environment where a female teenager could thrive. It's a difficult time for most people anyway, and to add adult issues to my plate was sometimes more than I could take. The ice rink was my escape. Journaling while listening to music was my escape. I guess I could say music was my escape. I was drawn to music I could emotionally relate to. I think that's where a lot of people who experience depression (which, in hindsight, I realize I encountered in those years) find solace—in music.

With that in mind, if it's difficult to jump right in and write out and label your loss and the emotions wrapped up in it, then ease into it. Find music that opens your heart a little. Soak in every word, feel the harmony within your soul, and if need be, cry. I have cried many times while listening to music—and do so to this day.

Music was such a huge influence for me growing up and still is. I tend to gravitate to music that matches my feelings in the moment. I still have sad days, and those are the days I choose a "soulful mix" on Spotify.

In fact, as I write, I often have a "deep focus" mix playing, which is filled with some of the most beautiful, inspiring sounds. Right now, "Archipelago Dreams" by Halcyon

Fields is playing. Without Spotify, I would likely never have heard this lovely song. These days, Spotify is my escape, my motivator, my focus-inducer, and my happiness engine when I feel like having a dance party.

Anything that helps evoke a positive feeling, and encourages an expression of those feelings, is a win in my book. Even when you are angry or frustrated, music can be an outlet for self-expression. Blast it loud and proud, move your body, work it out in the gym, or go for a run or fast-paced walk outside. Side note: it's difficult to be angry for too long when out in nature. The act of moving your body alone releases endorphins, and I think we can all agree that endorphins are a good thing. By the time you're done working the stress, frustration, and anger out, you may have forgotten what it was that upset you. Possibly, you maybe even arrive at a solution to your problem.

Mind-Centered vs. Heart-Centered Thinking

You may be asking yourself, "What in the world does listening to music, going for a walk or run, or being out in nature have to do with defining your grief?" For me, it had everything to do with my grief and still does today. Grief creates an elevated feeling of stress within the body. So, anything that can help release that will better enable you to cope with the grief itself, again, from a heart-centered place.

I've mentioned "heart-centered" before, and by that I mean coming from the deepest place within yourself; the place where all of your love (for yourself and others) is held. When we tackle our emotions from the mind alone, we may find relief for a time, but it's not long-lasting. At least, for me it wasn't.

At one point in adulthood, I sought out therapy. It was when my long-term relationship (where I hung my happiness hat) was coming to an end. Suddenly, I felt the emotional trauma of the past well up at once. But ya know, although I discovered the courage to end that relationship, I hadn't anticipated the emotional work that was yet to be done. This would really be my ticket to letting go. My emotional self was not addressed in therapy. I did not receive techniques (I've since discovered my own) to help me cope with all that came to the surface. It would be another thirteen years before I would know what I needed to do to maintain emotional balance—not just in my mind but within my heart-center…my soul.

Granted, this was only my personal experience with therapy. I should also mention that the type of treatment I had was hypnotherapy. It was a quick-n-dirty approach to get to the nitty-gritty issues. I remember leaving those sessions feeling emotionally and physically drained. Any emotional work I've ever done, though, has been emotionally and physically draining.

Writing this book has had me reliving certain aspects of my life all over again. Those old feelings still arise. And that's the message I want to share in this chapter: defining your grief enables you to recognize those feelings whenever they occur throughout your life, and I guarantee they will, especially in the circumstance of significant loss.

LABELING GRIEF

The difference today, though, compared to ten-plus years ago, is I am no longer enslaved to the emotions that kept me shackled for so many years. Back then, I would base every decision on what my mind wanted, because I never learned how to cope with the messages my heart was sending me. The heart-centered feelings that were at my core were the feelings that were a part of my soul. I couldn't make sense of any of it. It's just easier to react from a mind-view than it is from the heart-centered place that makes each and every one of us *who we are*. And when your mind-view is telling you you're shameful and not worthy over and over, you tend to believe it.

So, the question is this: when we start to recognize the difference between mind-centered vs. heart-centered, then what? And if you're still unsure how to distinguish between mind-centered and heart-centered, think of it as what we immediately desire resulting in impulsive behavior vs. what we truly know is right for us long term, even if it requires a bit of pain.

To put it in context, I'll use a relationship as an example. Your mind tells you that you don't like being alone. You've invested so much in this person and this relationship, and you've already been together this long. In a twisted way, you think keeping them in your life will eventually change *them*. Rather, what happens is it changes *you*—into someone you are not. Because we all know we can't make anyone change. We only have the power to change ourselves. And like a chameleon changes color to fit in with its surroundings, our minds will have us doing some ridiculous things, at times, to rationalize our mind-centered view of things.

Let's look at that same scenario coming from a heart-centered place, and more importantly, the place where intuition resides. Being able to take a bird's-eye view of the situation, separating one's self from the drama, and looking within, better equips us to make more confident decisions and likely sooner than we ever would if we relied solely on our mind's immediate response.

It is a powerful feeling when you know, in your heart of hearts, that what you are doing, every decision you are making, and every response to any given situation, is coming from a heart-centered space. We have an immediate mental reaction to every stimulus and feeling. In a minute fragment of time, we may not be able to change how we feel about something; however, we can very well change how we think about it. It takes an emotional process, though, to do so. Take inventory of how that event/person is making you feel in that moment, process it, ask why you're being triggered in that way, then change *how you think* about that event/person and move on. Then decide to let go of any emotional attachment to that event/person.

Discerning between the two is a skill no one can ever take from you and it can be developed over time. It starts with labeling what is keeping you stuck, then having the courage to step out of yourself; separating what your mind tells you from what you know deep in your heart, that which you long for…and deserve.

3

Death and Spirituality

"What causes night in our souls may leave stars."

- Victor Hugo

As tears welled up in my eyes, I received the bread of life—Jesus Christ, the body and giver of life itself—for the very first time. I was twenty-three. It was a life-changing event for me. In that moment and in the moments leading up to it, I reflected many times on my life before that day. I was overcome by the overwhelming feeling and steadfast belief that this experience is what the Lord had planned for me all along. I still hold this belief.

Without going into all the details of the differences between my Lutheran church experience and my conversion to Catholicism (and there are some distinct differences despite what some may believe), please understand I am only sharing my spiritual journey. My spiritual journey is the base of my grief experience and a vital part of my story.

I understand spirituality may not hold a place in your heart at the moment or maybe never has; only you know that truth. I simply ask, as you read these words within this chapter, that you keep in mind this is simply my experience, and I do not wish to push my beliefs onto you. I only want to give you a deeper understanding of how important spirituality became for me in my healing process.

Spirituality: Before and After Grief

Growing up, faith wasn't something I remember ever being discussed; certainly not after my father passed. I think my mother was angry that God would allow such a thing to happen to her and her children. That is the conclusion I came to at least, given the fact that *after* my father's funeral, we did not attend church on another Sunday, unless it was for a program we were taking part in for Sunday school or confirmation.

I can't even tell you, now, as I think back to confirmation class, if it was genuinely something I wanted to do. It's what my peers were doing, and I do know my mother encouraged it—for my own good. I do wish I'd had the ability then that I do now, to *feel* spiritual. It makes me wonder how different my early adult years might have been—how less challenging knowing myself might have been. I may not have become a lost sheep. Then again, I may not have arrived at the spiritual place I am at presently. I may still be going through the motions of *life experience* but not fully experiencing life *spiritually*.

I do have fond memories of our church life before grief knocked on our door. In fact, here is a photo of me combing my dad's hair, which I frequently did, as we were getting ready to go to church.

Typically, following church service, we would go to my maternal grandmother's for Sunday dinner. I have so many fond memories of that time, yet, when you're a child, adults underestimate what your child mind knows, understands, and remembers, no matter how vague those memories seem to be.

Grief can either strengthen your faith or shake it to its core. And maybe walking away and coming back to it is a natural part of the process for some people. Today, my mother is still a believer; however, practicing her faith in the traditional sense isn't something she does. And by "traditional sense,"

I mean that she doesn't attend church regularly. I honestly don't know what my mom still holds on to in her faith, and it's certainly a question which is important to ask after all these years. To this day, religion and spirituality aren't topics we typically discuss. I don't think it's because we would disagree; it's more of an unspoken understanding.

Whatever you believe happens once our soul or spirit departs our bodies is your own spiritual belief. Maybe the soul or spirit being separate from the body isn't something you believe at all. Discovering what it means to be spiritual and its purpose in our lives, for some, is a lifelong endeavor. For others, a tragic event takes place, or we reach a point in our lives where we finally become open to receiving love from others and more importantly, the love we *need* for ourselves.

When we don't feel worthy of love, it's difficult to give it to ourselves, much less those we say we love. Spiritual strength enables us to see love not as a commodity to be possessed, bargained for, or controlled, but as God intended— unconditional, for ourselves and others. I know we all struggle with this, sometimes our whole lives. When we realize there's a greater purpose to this earthly life, it opens us up to our heart-centered place. We see the desired destination is not here in the physical body, but rather, in "paradise," with our spiritual body.

The Dying Process

I have always been intrigued by the dying process. I'm sure having an early experience with death and dying made me naturally curious about that process. Regardless, I found myself, over the course of my youth and adulthood, drawn to a career in the medical field. As a teenager, I worked as a certified nursing assistant, and later in life I cared for adults receiving home health and hospice care. Once I learned the stages of dying, it amazed me how the body, as part of the natural course, and as God intended, gradually expired. To witness it time and time again never ceased to amaze me.

According to the website www.hospicenet.org, there are many physical signs the body gives that death is approaching. The following are such signs:

- Coolness—extremities may be increasingly cool to the touch and skin color may change. This indicates circulation of blood to extremities is decreasing and blood flow is being reserved for vital organs.

- Sleeping—increased amount of time sleeping, may be unresponsive and difficult to arouse. This is due to changes in the body's metabolism. I will add that it is important not to talk about the person like they are not there. It's best not to assume they cannot hear, as hearing is the last sense to be lost.

- Disorientation—confusion about the time, place, or the identity of those around them. This is also due to metabolism changes. During this time, it's best to identify yourself by name, speaking softly, clearly, and truthfully when communicating something important.

- Incontinence—loss of urine and/or bowel function as muscles in those areas begin to relax.

- Congestion—due to decreased fluid intake and an inability to cough up secretions, gurgling sounds coming from the chest are common. It is best to turn the person's head to the side rather than suctioning, as the latter will only increase secretion production.

- Restlessness—repetitive motions, such as pulling at bed or clothing or "picking" in the air is often due to decrease in oxygen circulation to the brain, as well as metabolism changes.

- Decrease in urine—urine output may become tea colored (indicating it's more concentrated) due to decreased fluid intake and circulation through the kidneys. During this time, it's common to need a catheter.

- Decreased food/fluid intake—decrease in appetite and thirst, wanting little or no food/fluid is the body's natural way of conserving energy. It's important not to force food/drink into a person. Rather, ice chips to refresh the mouth if able to swallow may be acceptable. Glycerin swabs are also used during this time to keep the mouth and lips moist and comfortable.

- Breathing pattern changes—irregular breathing, shallow breaths, and periods of no breathing for five seconds to a full minute are not uncommon. This is called Cheyne-Stokes breathing. Panting breathing is also common. All these indicate decreased circulation in the internal organs. Elevating the head and/or turning the person onto his/her side may bring comfort.

Unless prepared for or aware of such physical changes, they can seem disturbing to family and friends. It's emotionally difficult to watch your loved one not wanting to eat or drink for days at a time. And this is where, as a loved one watching from the sidelines, the aspect of having to eventually let go becomes more apparent.

Aside from the physical changes the body goes through to prepare for death, there are typical emotional, spiritual, and mental signs and symptoms of approaching death. Thinking back to my own experiences with loved ones and those I cared for who passed, this is the part that would grip the spiritual part of my heart. Because, until we get to that stage ourselves, it's a mystery what those who are dying are seeing, experiencing, and maybe even feeling. This stage, to me, is a beautiful mystery. It's a natural progression and preparation for a journey after this earthly life, about which we can only speculate.

According to the same website, typical emotional, spiritual, and mental signs and natural responses may be:

- Withdrawal—a person may seem unresponsive, withdrawn, or in a comatose state. This indicates preparation for release, a detaching from surroundings and relationships, and the beginning of letting go. Since hearing remains until the very end, identify yourself by name when you speak, hold his or her hand, and say whatever you need to say that will help the person let go.

- Vision-like experiences—it's not uncommon for the person to claim to have spoken to others who have already died or to see or have seen places not presently accessible or visible to you. This is not an indication of hallucinating or a drug reaction; rather, the person is beginning to detach from this life and is being prepared for the transition, so it will not be frightening. It is best not to contradict, explain away, or argue their claims. Rather, affirm his or her experience. This is normal and common and if your loved one seems frightened, explain this is a normal occurrence.

- Restlessness—the person may perform repetitive or restless tasks. This may indicate something is still unresolved or unfinished and is disturbing him or her, preventing him or her from letting go. It may be helpful to be a calming presence, helping to recall a favorite place or experience, read something comforting, or give assurance that it is OK to let go.

- Decreased socialization—at times, the person who is dying may want to only be with a very few people or even just one person. This is a sign of preparation for release and will help you know whose support is needed for the person to make the appropriate transition. You may or may not be a part of this inner circle. If not included, you may have fulfilled your task with your loved one, and it is time for you

DEATH AND SPIRITUALITY

to say goodbye. If you are a part of the final inner circle of support, the person needs your affirmation, support, and permission.

- Unusual communication—the person may make a seemingly out-of-character or odd statement, gesture, or request. This indicates that he or she is ready to say goodbye and is testing you to see if you are willing to let him or her go. Accept the moment as a beautiful gift when it is offered. Kiss, hug, hold, cry, and say whatever you most need to say.

- Giving permission—a dying person will generally try to hang on, even though it brings prolonged discomfort, to be sure those who are going to be left behind will be all right. Therefore, your ability to release the dying person from this concern and give him or her assurance that it is all right to let go whenever he or she is ready is one of the greatest gifts you have to give your loved one at this time.

- Saying goodbye—when the person is ready to pass on and you are able to let go, it is time to say goodbye. Do what feels right, in a comforting way, during this time.

I was not present at the time of my father's passing. He had reached the point in his health where my mother could no longer provide the around-the-clock care he required, so he was admitted to a nursing facility. A part of me always feels sad when I think about how young I was. Only because, had I been older, I would have really understood who my dad was. For me, it's always been this feeling of "never getting the chance."

So, it is my faith I cling to, that one day I *will* see him again. I would be lying if I didn't say I've had fantasies about what that will be like. It's not that I want to leave this earth now, in the present, it's only that I look forward to what the afterlife has in store.

What Does It Mean to Be Spiritual?

This brings up the question, how do you know you're going to heaven? I guess I don't; it's leading a faithful life that gives me hope that I will. Isn't that what spirituality is about as well—having faith? A feeling beyond comprehension and understanding that there is more to this life than our presence here on earth?

French philosopher Pierre Teilhard de Chardin said, "The physical body is not truly ours, it belongs to planet earth. We can call it our own while we reside in it, but it does not belong to us." This implies that we are, indeed, spiritual beings above all else. So, what is a "spiritual being"? Ask twenty people their definition of "spiritual being," and you'll likely get twenty different answers. We all view spirituality differently, and our upbringing, life experience, and maybe even personality can influence what we feel it means to be spiritual.

In the dictionary, a spiritual being is defined as "an incorporeal being believed to have powers that affect the course of human events." That's a pretty deep description, in my opinion. How can a spiritual being have powers that influence the course of human events? Consider for a moment, as you read this, that you are a believer in God and the Bible as the story of Jesus Christ's death and ultimate resurrection. Now, you may not, and that's entirely OK. Just open your mind briefly, if you will. What I believe is at the core of that definition is this: free will. Free will is the gift given to us by God. We all have it. We've been given the will to choose how we go about our lives every single day. So, with free will comes great power that affects the course of our lives.

18th century Swedish scientist/inventor/mystic Emmanuel Swedenborg says the natural and spiritual worlds co-exist. Acknowledged by the *Guinness Book of World Records* for having one of the highest IQs in history, Swedenborg has written more than thirty-five volumes on spiritual identity. He suggests that the natural world consists of everything you can see and, in contrast, the spiritual world consists of realities that we cannot see, such as heaven and hell. He believed that an individual's inner state can be reflected in their surroundings.

Nowadays, this belief that our outer world is a reflection of our inner selves would be regarded as "manifestation." I've read a lot about manifestation during my quest to understand my grief, to work out what it has cost me all these years, and to get a better understanding of who I am and why I do the things I do. The idea is that we manifest what is in our world through what we habitually tell ourselves within our minds. Regardless of what we tell ourselves, if it is the truth or not, our minds do not know the difference. Think about that for a moment. Your mind, by itself, apart from you, does not know the difference between what you are imagining and reality.

For example, if you close your eyes and imagine yourself going to a car lot and driving away with a brand new luxurious Lexus, what would that feel like? What would the car look like? What would it smell like? What would you see in your surroundings as you drive off the lot and hit the open road? Utilizing all five senses, close your eyes and imagine it. With intense focus, it can feel like it's really real. Lo and behold, you're sitting in your living room, no Lexus in your driveway, and not even the money in the bank account to buy one if you wanted to. This is the power of the mind, and it does not know the difference between a real, living experience and that which is imagined.

Now, imagine the role our minds play in our lives on a daily basis—what we *think* to be true, to what reality presents to us as truth. What I'm saying is this: what we believe to be truth is often skewed by our past. Is it any wonder that our spirituality can be skewed, too?

My mind told me for many years that my dad was a body in a coffin put six feet under and nothing more beyond that. Because at age eight, not having a developed spirituality, I believed that if God were a loving God, he wouldn't have let this happen to me. It's the message I heard around me as well. So then, where was HE in my life? That thought alone made me feel like a victim well into my adulthood.

Our slates are written in childhood. There are no do-overs, no second chances. What happens to us as children and how we are raised forever writes itself on the script of our lives. Our upbringing influences the things we tell ourselves when life is quiet around us. From the phrases, on repeat, within our minds when we look in the mirror to what we believe when faced with adversity. As well as how we respond to situations presented to us, and what we choose to do with our feelings as a result. This is my belief. While spirituality can feel like a dark place in our lives, it can also feel like the warmest, brightest light we crave or cling to, with which we re-write our script.

I encourage and implore you—look within long enough, act on inspiration when it calls to you, and be more curious about who you are and why you do the things you do. I have no doubt your eyes will open to the parts of yourself that need healing—spiritually and otherwise.

I have come a long way—from that eight-year-old girl who held so much sadness and anger inside and who resented God to the spiritually awakened soul I am today. Spirituality saved me. I believe, with all of my heart, it can save you from *yourself*, too. Where grief brings us to our knees, spirituality can lift us back up.

4

Living with and Resolving Grief

> *"The fact that grief takes so long to resolve is not a sign of inadequacy, but betokens depth of soul."*

- Donald Woods Winnicott

How do you live with and resolve your grief when you've been spiritually broken? Is it possible to move beyond sorrow?

In the midst of deep emotional pain, it's hard to see the light. I've had dark days many times, and I imagine there are many more to come. This is life. This is the experience God intended. How can we grow except through experience? How can we find ourselves, over and over, discovering what we're actually capable of, if we've never experienced pain? How can we find our way to the light and set in motion our unique spiritual journey without having felt so low that there's no way *but* up?

Maybe you are like me in that you are drawn to stories of underdogs. Perhaps you, too, appreciate stories of triumph in the face of adversity. I think in some ways, empathy grows from sorrow. How can we possibly put ourselves in the shoes of another? We can't. However, if we are able to *relate* our story and ourselves, in some way, to the circumstances of another, we begin to *feel* differently towards the other. As a result, compassion blooms.

To See and to Be Seen

Deep, heart-centered compassion beams from someone like a ray of sunshine. When you are hurting, and someone is looking in your eyes and actually understands you and is present in that moment with you—you just know. They get it. Maybe they didn't experience something similar, but they've grieved, felt lost, felt broken—and yet, *they see you*. Isn't that what we all want in this human experience: to be seen and heard? We hush our voices, we play small, we allow the nagging voices in our minds to dictate our choices…our free will.

Instead of waiting for someone to see us, how about we see ourselves? To do that, we have to show up to this human experience for ourselves before we can show up for anyone else. We cannot give to others what we cannot give to ourselves. I found this challenging in my healing process, especially at first.

So, what does showing up for yourself look like? It's consciously living, choosing to make *you* a priority. I neglected myself and my well-being once I had children.

Before that, I neglected my emotional well-being. Having children has a way of taking everything you know about life and flipping it on its side, causing you to grow in the process. It is in growing with my children that I saw the parts of myself I could no longer hide from. With every reaction of anger or fear towards my kids, a pattern arose, and only recently have I had some serious aha! moments where I am able to better understand where I have fallen short for my children. Because really, growth is an ongoing, forever process.

Every event, sorrow, joy, milestone, curveball of life thrown at us, and every soul that crosses our path holds within it a lesson. Some people may feel they are gluttons for punishment. That is victim mindset rearing its ugly head. Does this sound familiar? "Things like this *always* happen to me and nobody else!" I am starting to believe it's because life has a way of knocking us on the head over and over and over until we get it. There is something we need to learn to grow and expand our consciousness.

Living Consciously

Consciousness was not a part of my vocabulary until 2014. I tortured myself that entire year. I wrestled with the unrest I felt within myself. All the personal transformation stories I've heard and read throughout the past two-and-a-half years had one thing in common: the storyteller (myself included) could pinpoint when they realized, finally, *this* (whatever *this* is; it is unique for everyone) is not working. Then, they worked on figuring it out and did something about it. You have to reach a point where you tell yourself, "I'm absolutely tired of being tired—of living life, going through the motions, and not being present for myself or those I love."

I spent an entire year working on myself. I went to great lengths to better understand my past, the decisions I had made, how things turned out, what influenced me, the person I was when I was growing up and who my children have grown me into. I sought out a life coach. I had a hand analysis, which clearly expresses how lost I felt, thinking the answers to my prayers were in my hands. Although hand analysis helped me to understand aspects of myself, I was digging for something I was never going to find in my hands. I also journaled like mad. I read self-help books, purchased a self-help program by renowned life coach and author Tony Robbins, and sought to deepen my spiritual faith by listening to Bible scripture via a free Bible app (available on iTunes). I read, and continue to read, *Living Faith*, which is a quarterly booklet of daily scripture readings and writings from various authors.

The truth is, I was a lost soul—lost from that day when I was eight years old. It has taken me nearly thirty years to find myself; the me I was created to be. Despite it all, I believe this is the path that was paved for me. I craved more from my life. I knew I had more in me to give the world and was restless because I didn't know what "giving to the world" looked like *for me*.

In 2014, I decided to close my photography studio, which I lovingly labored over and put everything I had into, after six years in business. I know now that the business blossomed out of the desire within me to prove something to myself. Having been an introvert, unless I had some "liquid courage," and always being the creative type that loved a challenge, a photography business seemed like a fun thing to "try on." I'd had all three of my children by this time, the youngest only six months old. I can say now that nothing in life grows you more than tragedy, the military, parenthood, and being an entrepreneur. I had experienced all four by the time I was thirty years old.

My point in sharing this is not to toot my own horn, but rather to express how many times in my life I sought to find myself and how many times I failed to look within myself. I know I still have a lot of "figuring out" to do—my personal development work never ends. The day I stop trying to improve upon myself is the day I am dead. I have made it my mission, it seems, to figure myself out.

Going through this self-discovery process, I've become increasingly curious about others and their stories. In a time where we feel as though we're going it alone, suffering in silence, and rising to a new day without a feeling of purpose, I felt compelled to share what I had learned. This led me to start a blog about personal growth (www.theguidedheart.com), where I share snippets of my experiences, as well as resources that have helped me along my own spiritual/personal development quest for more joy (and purpose) in my life.

We have so much to learn from each other. Because we exist at the same time, on this earth, there is an opportunity for growth and understanding all around us. We have opportunities every day to *see* each other, to grow with one another, and share our experiences and stories. Why go through this life feeling alone?

There are plenty of people out there today who are very familiar with sorrow or grief. If you are a parent like me, then you also face the challenge of parenting; living what can sometimes feel like the "daily grind" we call life. We *are* all in this together, as cliché as it may sound, because we face similar challenges. Stack this on top of our unique emotional and spiritual experience, and it can make life feel overwhelming at times. The golden ticket is to realize that it's not what we do that defines us. It is how we see ourselves that changes how we see our world around us. When we rise above ourselves and all the stories hidden within us, we grow.

Rather than resigning ourselves to the fact that we will forever live in our sorrow no matter what we do, let's instead accept that grief is a journey, of the spiritual kind as well as the personal development kind. My journey took nearly thirty years and maybe that's why I felt called to write this book. In fact, I believe that is the very reason.

Two years ago, when I started my blog, I also had the inspired thought to write a book that would be written for widows/widowers who were left to raise young children. Basically, the kind of book I wish my mom had read. It would have been written from my perspective as an adult, looking back on my childhood experience with grief and providing a "what to do, what not to do" to help your children through the grieving process. I sat on that idea up until just four weeks ago (January of this year, 2017).

Had I started that book two years ago, it would not have been the right time. I was still in the midst of my own personal growth and, as I know now, I had much to learn. Also, I think that book just would not have been the *right* book to write— at least not at the time. My story of grief wasn't quite over, as just this past year, I reconnected with my father's brother, as well as cousins I haven't seen since the day of my dad's funeral. I had more healing to come, and two years ago I didn't know it. So, it is with perfect, divine timing that I sit and type out these words today.

The Mind-Body Connection with Grief and Suffering

As my story goes on, so will my growth, spiritually and emotionally. Physically, grief took its toll. There is one author in particular who articulates the mind-body connection so beautifully, and that is Louise Hay. I read her book, *You Can Heal Your Life*. In the book, Louise shares her story of being sexually abused at age five, and the continual physical abuse she suffered until her teens, at which time she had had enough and ran away from home. She was later diagnosed with cancer in the vaginal area (not surprising, given her previous trauma), and decided to take matters into her own hands and start, for the first time, her healing journey from childhood to her present-day diagnosis. She never had surgery. Instead, with a holistic approach, changing her diet, adding in reflexology, and doing affirmation work, she healed herself of cancer—again, without surgery. She realized that disease can be "healed" if we are willing to change the way we think, believe, and act.

I never believed in the mind-body connection more than after experiencing my own health issues, which, coincidentally, began in 2012 and continued off and on through 2015. What I have come to realize is that when I was experiencing bowel issues, vitamin deficiencies, worsened anemia, appetite changes, etc., it was directly related to a stressful and/or emotionally challenging time in my life. Being filled with daily anxiety about what I was going to do with my life (in 2014), and feeling this immense desire for more but not knowing where to start, and also not feeling confident in my own abilities, manifested in my health and well-being in a negative way.

Finally, in 2015, I began to come to this realization after doing much personal work, and decided to make some changes. Personal wellness is a conscious decision I have to make on a daily basis, whether it be physical exercise, emotional release by journaling/listening to music/reading God's word/writing, or mental challenge by learning something new like acoustic guitar or hand lettering. Actively creating on a daily basis is what I found truly feeds my soul, and, in turn, benefits my overall well-being and spiritual self. Once I got to a space of ease and began going with the ebb and flow of life (letting go of the need to control outcomes), things began to fall into place. I landed a job that fits my personality perfectly and works around my life, not the other way around. I have experienced more inspired thought than I know what to do with, and feel, for the first time ever, the parts of me that were broken for so long have been healed.

Take the parts of this chapter as you need or see fit. I know spirituality is a heavy subject and how each person grieves varies. If you decide you are ready to start healing your brokenness, I invite you to check out the resources I mentioned. Please remember, grief exists because love exists. The goal is to be able to be fully accepting of love for ourselves and for others, to give it back to the world, unconditionally. Every day is a work in progress. We never fully "arrive," but consciously making a choice to try will make all the difference in your life.

PART II:

The Long-Term Effects of Grief

5

The Victimization of Grief

> *"There is no such thing as a problem without a gift for you in its hands.*
> *You seek problems because you need their gifts."*

- Richard Bach

This March (2017), it is thirty years since my father passed away. As I mentioned before, I feel as though this book is perfect timing. In the thirty years since, my grief has never gone away. I don't expect it ever will.

The thing with grief is, it comes and goes. There are moments where I am overcome with emotion, and not just from the loss itself, but from my life experience because of it. It's hard to get over the thought that if *that* hadn't happened, then *this* ("this" meaning all the negative experiences) wouldn't have happened. It comes back to reconciling your grief and learning to live with it. I'm not certain this is possible if the constant replay in your mind is "Why did this happen to me?" And this brings me to the "victim mindset" and how grief itself can feel like a downward spiral of "Why me?"

The Stages of Grief

In her 1969 book *On Death and Dying*, a Swiss psychiatrist, Elisabeth Kubler-Ross, inspired by her work with terminally ill patients, describes the five most common experiences the terminally ill go through from diagnosis to death. She would later expand and apply this research to include the bereaved and those who suffer losses of various kinds as well.

The five stages, which may or may not be experienced and if so, may not be in this order, are: denial, anger, bargaining, depression, and acceptance. For explanation purposes, I will define these as they apply to someone who is grieving, as opposed to someone being diagnosed with a terminal illness. As Kubler-Ross expressed in her research, the stages may be similar.

- **Denial**: Clinging to false, preferable reality.
- **Anger**: Recognizing denial can't continue; may become frustrated towards those closest, expressing feelings of "Why me?" "This isn't fair." "Why would this happen?" The need to want to blame someone.
- **Bargaining**: Hope that grief can be avoided, seeking compromise, feelings of "I'd give anything to have them back."

- **Depression**: Ongoing mourning, becoming silent, not wanting visitors, feelings of "Why bother?" "This hurts so badly, why go on?"
- **Acceptance**: Embracing mortality, the future is inevitable, feelings of "It's going to be okay." "It is what it is."

Do you relate to any of these stages? I know I do. I also recognize these steps in others who have loved and lost or have gone through emotionally trying times.

I did not have an understanding of my father's diagnosis or what it meant when he received it, two years prior to his death. I also don't recall being told what was inevitably to come (his impending death). I was sheltered from my own reality. I suppose, at the time, my mother thought she was protecting me.

I can tell you, today, having been through what I have, if I were faced with this situation with my husband while raising our children, they would be made entirely aware of what was going on. I would want to be completely transparent with our kids.

Maybe you're reading this right now and being faced with such a circumstance. If so, know my heart is with you. I have you in mind as I write these words. It comes back to hindsight. So, let me offer you mine, with the hope that it can help you.

Keeping your children in the dark may feel like you're protecting them. I know it does. As previously mentioned, I believe my mother did what she thought was right at the time—protecting me. I knew my father was sick. I saw the colostomy bag. I smelled the smell when he changed it. To this day, I remember it—everything about it. And yet, I was unaware of what was to come. Would it have changed anything at my age? I don't know. What I do know is that I woke up one day, went to school, and from that day forward I was made aware there would never again be a place set for him at the table. It was a finality that was so abrupt, yet it wasn't. It was abrupt to me only because I was kept in the dark.

Therefore, I don't believe I experienced any of these stages until after the fact, ongoing for years at various stages of my life. That's the tricky part of grief in childhood. You can't understand unless you're reading these words and can say, "This happened to me too as a child." Childhood grief is different than emotional trauma at other stages. I confidently say that because I've experienced pain both as a child and as an adult (although fortunately I've been through nothing similar to my father's death as an adult—not yet anyway). My mother is still living; however, I know the grief I experience upon her passing will be very different than that I experienced when I lost my father.

I was a victim of grief as a child. Not by my own understanding, as I did not have the mental capacity I do now. Back then, it was me trying to make sense of it all and not really knowing if I was. As I mentioned, there was no therapy provided to me at the time. The "truths" I grew up with were those I conjured up in my own mind and those that were told to me, or I heard. This state of confusion continued for many years. And this is what is so frustrating for me, and what could easily make me feel victimized all over again, time and time again: how different my life could have been.

Adapting to Grief

Because grief never goes away and only changes, you must learn to adapt to it. Coincidentally (or not coincidentally—I'm not sure), *adaptability* happens to be my number one strength, according to Tom Roth's book *Strengths Finder 2.0*. In the book, instructions are provided for taking an online assessment of your personality traits.

You may be asking yourself, "Why would you even want to take such an evaluation?" In short, becoming an entrepreneur is what catapulted my desire to become the best version of myself possible. Entrepreneurship has a way of stretching and testing you further than you thought was possible. Becoming your own boss makes you show up for yourself in ways you never imagined and teaches you many valuable lessons along the way.

As a result, my entrepreneurship journey brought up a lot of old baggage and became the tipping point for years of lack of self-reflection. I think self-reflection is one of the unspoken gifts of entrepreneurship. When we self-reflect, we learn and grow. Little did I know how much growing I had left to do. My entrepreneurship journey is for another book. However, for me and my personal development and healing journey, it's what got the ball rolling. For you, it may be something entirely different.

Back to adaptability and its importance when it comes to talking about grief: it's not a matter of dismissing or ignoring your feelings revolving around emotional trauma. Rather, it's about getting into the driver's seat of your life—with grief in the backseat. You may take it with you wherever you go, acknowledging its presence, but letting the feelings move through you—a natural ebb and flow. Recognizing, accepting, and releasing as you go. Surrender and acceptance both lead to a lighter feeling.

Ah…letting go. I mention that a lot. It's become my mantra for life. So much so, I have it tattooed on the inside of my right wrist—*Let go Let God*. My spirituality has been at the forefront thus far, in how I write and the words I choose. My spirituality is one thing that has helped me in being able to let go of all the worry and thoughts surrounding anything or anyone in my life that I can neither change nor control. It is a losing battle to think you can. Therefore, I acknowledge, accept, and let go of that thought entirely. There is only one mind I can control—my own.

Letting go and adaptability go hand and hand, I suppose. First, when you acknowledge your feelings around grief, you may shrug them off or stuff them down, as I did for a long time. In a way, you could say this is adapting to your emotion. You modify your behavior based on your feelings. If you stuff your feelings down, you can guess it will have a negative impact. So, adapting can look both positive and negative. What will move you forward, however, is leaning into positivity. To do that, you must sit with and work through all that troubles your heart and negatively impacts your physical and mental health and well-being.

What I encourage you to ask yourself is: would you rather be a chameleon and fake it, or would you rather learn to adjust to what is, so that eventually you can let go? My mother never faked it in front of me. I never had to guess how she was feeling—ever. I guess you could say she wears her heart on her sleeve. She also rarely filtered (and still doesn't) what she said. Despite that, I still don't recall ever knowing the truth about the situation before my dad's death. Again, it may have been talked about in the open, and I may have just blocked it out. I can only recall my feelings of that time, and I only remember that I wished I could fix him and make him better. In fact, there's a picture I have, wearing a mask and blue hair cover and all, where I am playing "doctor," thinking I could do just that.

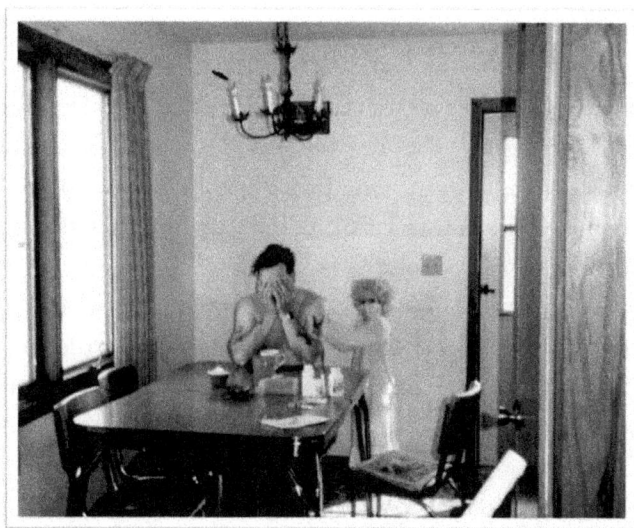

Stuck in the In-Between

So, what do you do when you're caught in that space between where you know you can't change what has happened (acceptance) and you feel as though life itself is a daily struggle (depression)? That is a challenging position to be in. Honestly, I think my own mother was stuck here well into my adulthood. You know you can't change what *is*, just as what *was* cannot be altered. And yet, every damn day feels like a reminder of what was and what is, and it's painful—every single day. If years are dragging on, and your sadness and hopelessness about the situation aren't going anywhere, then it's time to take action. I am not going to tell you that you can heal your depression. I'm not going to tell you that eventually, it will just go away and the sun will rise, and you'll suddenly find life bright again. I, myself, sought therapy. There is absolutely nothing wrong with that. And sometimes, we just can't do it alone.

Which brings me to this fact: we victimize ourselves over and over again when we have this idea in our minds that something is wrong with us, when simply, we only loved. It sounds absurd reading that, doesn't it? But, isn't that the root of it? We beat ourselves up because we care so much, almost as if it's a sense of regret at times. "Why did I let myself love if it was going to feel like this when I lost it?" That is the risk in life we take, with everything and everyone we bring into our lives. A beautiful risk, if you ask me.

We victimize ourselves again if we allow that pain to guard us against feeling love again—love of another, love of career, love of life itself—because, on a dime, it all can change again and the rug can be swept from underneath us—*yet again*. This is the cycle of the victimization of grief. It's that old saying, "history repeats itself." Unless we break the cycle (and the hold) being a victim has over us. We have to choose to decide to drive out, like the Cheryl Strayed quote states.

How Not to Be a Victim of Grief

Can you escape victim mentality entirely? I believe it's *mostly* possible, meaning that eventually, with the exercises and resources shared, you will learn how to recognize it and be able to get out of it more quickly and not remain stuck there.

Personal development and working on yourself takes work. No wonder people tend to avoid this like the plague! We get stuck on auto-pilot and go about life numbly, never allowing ourselves to feel those icky feelings we only feel in snippets because we're so preoccupied in our minds with the daily grind of life. Progress takes time, and working on yourself is an investment of time; the best investment you can ever make. So, let's get to work!

There are three core steps I have found beneficial for myself in my own self-work. I would also add that having a simultaneous spiritual journey was highly beneficial. However, I don't think that's necessarily universal for everyone (although studies have shown that those who have a core religious or spiritual belief system are simply happier).

First, ask yourself better questions. For example, look in the mirror and ask yourself, "Would I want to be around me?" Pay attention to the answer that comes to you at that moment. Often, to put it bluntly, people who are stuck in a victim role are not fun people to be around. People don't come to you to be lifted up, encouraged, and laugh. You can't do that for yourself when you're in that mindset, much less for others. So, acknowledging what is, is your first step.

Then, ask yourself if it is true. Continue to ask yourself better questions: "Does everyone avoid me?" If you can't find evidence of that, then maybe this is a "truth" you only tell yourself in your own mind. What proof can you find, if any? On the other hand, there may be plenty of people who want to be around you, you just tend to push them away. So, figuring out which it is, is key. It starts by asking yourself better questions and digging and digging for the facts.

I'm reminded of The Work, a self-assessment tool created by Byron Katie. This work typically focuses on relationships, but I think the most important relationship is the one within ourselves, as every other relationship flows *from* us.

You have to be able to separate your thoughts from fact, continuing to ask yourself questions like, "Do I absolutely know it's true?" or "How do I react when I believe this thought?" and "Who would I be without this thought?" Once you've answered the better questions, you find a turnaround for each one. For example, for the statement "Nobody wants to be around me," the turnaround would be "I don't like to be around me." Is this turnaround as true or more true than the original thought? Then find examples of how it is true. One example could be, "I find the negative in every situation." Try to find three turnarounds for every statement you believe to be true after asking yourself the four core questions:

1. Is it true? Yes or No. If no, move to number 3.
2. Can you absolutely know that it's true? Yes or No.
3. How do you react, what happens, when you believe that thought?
4. Who would you be without the thought?

Before we can change behavior, we must first acknowledge it. It's a testament I will likely repeat over and over.

Second, keep a journal. I mentioned this before, and I'll probably say it again, but getting your thoughts onto paper takes away their power. Thoughts become things, and if you keep the same thoughts on replay in your mind, it's tough for your mind to distinguish what is truth from what is the truth *you're telling yourself.*

Third, reflect on what you've written and write some more. Once we understand why we do what it is we do, and why we are the way we are, we are better equipped to change our thought patterns. Thoughts become things, remember?

If you find you need more help in getting clear on where you want to be in life, maybe it's not a therapist you need; maybe a life coach is the answer to help you get past those mental blocks. My life coach was instrumental in my personal growth. I don't seek counsel from her now, but we do keep in touch as I consider her a friend. And that's the thing, sometimes our friends or family are not the best people to seek advice from as they are too close to us. An outsider perspective can be very beneficial and enlightening.

Grief almost seems to rewire our brains. Continual emotional trauma, whether due to one event or various emotional traumas that we continue to replay in our minds, deprives us of joy. We all know the old saying, "laughter is the best medicine," right? There's scientific proof to back this up. So, what I'm pondering is: chronic emotional trauma can have the same effect but in the opposite way. Imagine if this goes on for years! No wonder working on ourselves takes an enormous amount of effort and time.

Most of us get to where we are in our lives over time, not overnight. Isn't it sensible to think, then, that self-work is, and always will be, work in progress? We never "arrive" at our best selves, but we can strive every day to be the best version of ourselves, no matter what life may throw our way.

6

The Cost of Being a Victim to Grief

> *"One of the hardest lessons in life is letting go.*
> *Whether it's fear, anger, guilt, betrayal, or loss…*
> *We fight to hold on, and*
> *we fight to let go."*

- Author Unknown

How many years will you allow to go by before you decide to pull back the curtains and let the sun shine, metaphorically, in your life and within your soul?

Opening the Door to My Past

Nearly thirty years went by in my own life where I felt like I kept a part of myself in the past. Interestingly, it would take an unplanned, unforeseen event to bring that part back into the present, forcing me to deal with it and let it go.

I briefly mentioned it previously, but I am referring to

finding out my father's only living brother (my uncle who I hadn't spoken to or seen since my dad's funeral) is terminally ill with brain cancer. It became a matter of now or possibly never, and that's when I decided to go see him in the hospital.

Walking in, I did not know what to expect, how he would react, how I would be received, or even if he would recognize or remember me (considering his illness). To my surprise, it didn't take him long to see me as that little girl he remembered me to be. We embraced, cried, and just being there in his presence brought so much overwhelming comfort to me.

During our conversation, my uncle mentioned that one of his daughters and his niece (one I hadn't seen since the funeral in 1987 and the other I didn't remember meeting) were coming the following day for the long weekend. His niece was driving cross-country, and on the way stopping at his daughter's, where they would travel the remainder of the trip together. You can imagine my surprise when there's a knock on the door, and they walk in! It was yet another overwhelming surprise. They appeared equally surprised to see me after all these years.

We hugged, cried, and had a great chat the rest of the evening. We ended the night by going out for dinner, then parted ways and shared our intentions to keep in touch.

On my drive home I reflected on the overwhelming feeling I had and the nervousness I felt as I traveled to see my uncle. I also recall feeling as though an emotional weight had been lifted, and my heart had been opened. It was a visit I will never forget. Taking that chance changed me at that moment and, in an instant, had a positive impact on my life.

Am I opening myself up to more sadness? Absolutely, as I do not know how much time my uncle has left. Just when I decided to open up the door to my past, it will be closed on me, whether I like it or not. I try not to think about it, but I know it will be yet another experience with grief all over again.

I have allowed so much time to go by that I can't get back. That thought alone makes me feel sadness—an overwhelmingly heavy feeling of regret. If there is one lesson I've learned from my grief, it is to live without regret.

Having regret is definitely a part of grief. The one left behind thinks about all the things they never got to say, the things they wish had been said when they had the opportunity, or maybe even things that were said that they wish they could take back. I'm not sure which regret is worse. Regardless, I think the takeaway is this: take advantage of every opportunity you can to speak your heart. Never let others doubt your love for them.

Can you see where the feeling of regret can cause you to replay scenarios in your mind? And when we do this, we're reminding ourselves over and over of the things that *should* have, *could* have...you *wish* had been said. It leads us down the rabbit hole of more despair and ultimately only adds to the role of being a victim of grief. It's easy to remain in a "victim of grief" mindset, but it's a struggle to get out of it.

Again, I'll remind you that I was stuck in that place for the majority of my adult life. I wrote this book to share with you, however, that it doesn't have to be that way.

Trust, Faith, and Everything Between

From childhood, I received messages that this world is a cruel place and to trust few people. You're better off standing on your own two feet and counting on no one but yourself and your immediate family. I listened, and it was as if the universe heard, providing me with proof to not trust others time and time again. When I felt what love was for the first time at seventeen, I was told I was wrong and didn't know what love was. Well into adulthood, I would question the world around me on a daily basis. I held people under a microscope. I guarded my feelings, only sharing them with my journal. I never dared to speak of hopes and dreams— that's what dreamers do. So, instead, I daydreamed of my "somedays" in my own mind. And looking back, my own mind was as much my prison as it was my escape.

I share this with you not to display some sort of pity-me story, but to give you a snapshot of what the victim mindset looks like when it's expressed to others and the effect it can have on those around you.

It is a sobering thought, even for myself as I write these words, how, in some way, I could have expressed these same ideas towards my own children. I know it is not with intent, as much as it wasn't the intent of my mother; however, when you are in a victim mindset, you don't see the damage it causes to yourself and those around you.

Does everyone who grieves fall into the victim mindset? I think for a time, only because it's natural to feel as though losing someone you love (or that career, limb, eyesight, health, etc.) was done *to* you. But, I don't believe everyone who grieves in their life stays in that mindset.

What I have found to be the difference for myself, which is also the one thing I recognize as the difference for others I know who have grieved, is faith. And not even necessarily religious faith, but this unshakable faith, trust, and acceptance that what happened *happened*, it cannot be undone, but if you *believe* that this world is a supportive place then ultimately, you will be OK. It is blind faith, in a way.

When you grow up learning not to trust the world around you, not to have faith that the world works (or God works, if you're spiritual) for your greater good, you spend years expecting the other shoe to drop. It is a learned behavior not to trust or have faith in others and the world around you. When you grow up not feeling supported, your shoulders have to become mighty broad to tolerate the weight of feeling as though you're going it alone. That is a very lonely road to be on and one that adds to the victim mindset.

Imagine for a moment what it has cost you to remain a victim of your circumstances. Relationships—because you didn't trust. Faith—because you didn't trust. Friendships— because you didn't trust. Money—because, well, you didn't trust it will be there next week or next month. You are not only in a victim mindset but in the mindset of *lacking* as well. And who is the first person to get the blame for all of these thoughts that swirl in your mind? Well, everyone else, of course. Until you flip the switch and realize that you, and you alone, put those exact thoughts in your own mind. No one else can possibly do that but you. I don't believe anyone can dispute that.

Victim mindset is a fascinating subject to me. I think so much of the hurt in this world today stems from humanity passing on this "trait," I'll call it, to future generations. We "condition" ourselves to point the finger at the world around us when things go awry, when in actuality, our own minds convince us the world around us is to blame for our own despair and demise.

Those that served our country during the Great Depression are said to be the "Greatest Generation." I think about the conditions in which they lived and the lack they experienced on a daily basis. Do you think they wallowed in their tears and felt sorry for themselves? I imagine, during those times, women did. Naturally, as a mother, if you're not sure how you'll feed your family their next meal, surely you feel enormous despair at times.

Imagine for a moment if this were to happen today. Can you imagine the disarray? I even hate to imagine it, as my imagination paints a very dark image of feast and famine—survival of the fittest. I think about the tenacity of those during the Great Depression era, though, and their ability to not just survive but *thrive* during that time. They overcame then what most today would possibly view as the end of the world. I don't believe victim mindset had a place back then. They knew what needed to be done and did it.

I use this example only to illustrate my point that throughout history there have been periods of great sadness and unfortunate circumstances for many, and yet those people overcame these insurmountable odds. What makes them different? It's a question I, myself, can't answer. On the other hand, maybe it's an example we can hold against our own lives and realize, ya know, things aren't so bad, it could *always* be worse. Indeed. Just *maybe* then, optimism, like victim mindset, can be learned. And, like a muscle, it can be built up and strengthened.

The many negative events in my life, stacked up on top of one another, only added to my ability (and yes, I say ability because it's a frame of mind we practice daily) to remain a victim of my circumstances. Recall when I talked about mind-centered thinking vs. heart-centered thinking in chapter two. The frame of mind I was stuck in that kept me in that victim mindset was mind-centered thinking. It is this fight-or-flight response in our minds; the quick, automatic response where we don't acknowledge our hearts long enough to attune ourselves to heart-centered thinking. It's the very place where empathy, trust, and faith evolve and grow. Rather, our thoughts fluidly flow from one hemisphere to the other, and we pass judgment on those thoughts within a split second, and in that split second it becomes our truth—*in our minds.*

Look in the Mirror

And so, passive living is the cost of being stuck in a victim mindset. We don't actively seek what is in our own hearts. We re-live pain after pain in our minds. With every negative event that occurs, it's as if our judgments and thoughts are solidified. Suddenly, our thoughts take on the persona equal to that of a mother scoffing at her rebellious teenager getting herself into trouble, as if to say, "See, I told you so—you never listen to me." It's as if our thoughts manifest in our lives exactly what it is we'd like to scream at the world around us, and the universe gives us every lesson we need to learn in the most painful way possible.

It simply does not have to be this way. We pay a mighty price for not looking in the mirror and declaring that enough is enough. Thoughts are just that, and they can be changed. Changing a pattern isn't easy. It is a daily practice to become more mindful of the words within our own minds. Mindfulness—yes, yet another step on the ladder of moving on from grief. It's so important, there is a chapter devoted to it later in this book.

In the meantime, go back to where you initially wrote down all the ways in which you've experienced grief. I hope you also took some time to journal the feelings that came up for you when you thought about that grief; where you've been and how far you've come in your own grief journey. Reflect now, if you will, on what you think you've missed out on. Granted, grief does not have a timeline and everyone, literally everyone, grieves differently and goes through the

stages (and maybe not even all stages) of grief at different times. The idea, though, is: if you are currently stuck in grief, just thinking about how it is sucking away the joy in your life can sometimes jolt you into inspired action.

If you are feeling emotionally stuck, reflecting on what you're missing out on (or have missed out on) in life may bring forth mixed emotions. These feelings may be even more painful than the grief itself and may be enough to *make* you want to change your pattern of thinking and ultimately, your way of living.

Living in grief day after day, year after year, isn't living. Claim to be a survivor of grief but then use that as a reminder to demand more *living* today, not someday. Refusing to explore this possibility for yourself will, without a doubt in my mind, cost you—if you choose to remain a victim to grief. I know what it has cost me.

To move forward, I've had to learn how to let a lot of mental baggage go. Otherwise, it is a vicious cycle of grief, regret, and more grief. Break the cycle before more time passes, for those in your life and more importantly for yourself. When *you* take care of *you*, everyone in your life benefits.

7

Grief Changes You

> "We all want our grief validated…
> We don't want people to fear it nor try to fix it —
> just acknowledge it."

\- Necole Stephens

Grief changes a person in ways one may not expect. One of the things I've noticed for myself and people I've talked to on this subject is that your capacity to empathize increases after grief.

Once you go through a really trying and challenging time, your view of the world shifts a bit. Although you may be overcome with grief, you are, possibly for the first time, able to empathize and sit with others in their own grief. Suffering brings out in us the capacity to feel the suffering of others.

Why? Because we know what emotional pain feels like. It is a quality in myself I would not change. The flip side of this is that I feel, sometimes too often, the pain of others. I can feel others' pain so deeply that at points in my life, the circumstances of others (typically those closest to me) and the emotional turmoil they were going through would affect me so profoundly it would affect my own health and well-being.

A Survivor in the Making

I relate to suffering and emotional pain. So, if anyone comes to me, I am present, in their pain with them. And indeed, this has affected my marriage at times. I can remember several occasions throughout my marriage where I was an emotional wreck. I would begin to neglect myself, not showering for two to three days at a time, consumed by the thoughts of those currently in my life who were suffering. I would get mad for allowing myself to get so overwhelmed by the suffering of others, but lo and behold, the same thing would happen again and again.

"Why do I put myself through this?" I thought. I wish I knew. What I do know is that I am not alone. There must be others who have experienced suffering of all kinds throughout life, and it is just woven into the fabric of our very being—to simply *feel* deeply. So, I have come to accept this aspect of myself; however now, later in life, I am better able to recognize when I'm starting to slip too far down the emotional rabbit hole.

How about you? Have you found yourself in similar situations but never connected your own suffering to the suffering of others? I've talked a lot about grief with a negative undertone; rightfully so, as it disrupts everything we come to know and believe in this life. It brings everything into question. Feelings bubble to the surface we've never dealt with, and maybe there are parts of ourselves we despise that grief helps us to recognize, even as we do our very best to hide them away from others.

On the other hand, pain and suffering bring out love and care for others we never knew we had the capacity to have. This love and attention isn't like the bond between siblings, mother-daughter, or parent and child; it's different. It's the kind of love that makes you *see* suffering in the world differently. Maybe even for the first time in your life, feeling what it may feel like to be in another person's shoes. And that, my friends, is one of the gifts grief and suffering gives us.

I believe being able to put yourself in the shoes of another is a gift—not for you, but for those around you. It's a gift for the stranger you pass on the street. It's a gift from within you that you can share with the world in every human interaction you have.

For example, say you're in line at the checkout at a busy supermarket and you can see the cashier is noticeably bothered and unhappy. You can imagine what her day must have been like to this point and empathize as opposed to adding your impatience to her day. Maybe you even imagine that, on the inside, she too is suffering—even if you have no idea. Doing so shifts your mindset in that moment from one of impatience, upset you're stuck behind someone who is slower than molasses, to one of empathy.

I would often think that I was a magnet for moments like this. There was a period of time in my life where I felt like the universe was constantly using me in a social experiment and I was constantly being tested, because who gets so unlucky? I found myself in situations just like this so many times in my life, and still do from time to time.

Recently, I had to get my son two hours away for a basketball tournament. Somehow, some way, I got to exactly where I needed to be with a tire going flat and another tire with a nail in it. The odds were clearly against me. However, what tested my patience was dealing with a roadside assistance company that ended up being zero help. They called and indicated someone wouldn't be able to come help until the next day. Coincidentally, this happened on the thirtieth anniversary of my father's death. In that moment, I was focused on gratitude—for my son and me arriving safely, despite the odds of having two compromised tires. This also happened where I was surrounded by friends who could help me.

What I've realized is this: I had this reoccurring thought in my mind that I was not a patient person. It was as if the world around me set out to prove to me that I actually was patient.

Needless to say, I no longer say I am impatient. I have accepted that I can't control the world around me. I can't make others do what I want them to do, no matter how hard I will it to happen. I accept that everything happens around me, to me, and for me in the right time, space, and sequence, and trust that I am fully supported in life. That everything that happens is for my greater good. This is a massive shift from where I was even just five years ago.

Imagine how different your life would be right now if you too had that shift, believing that everything that happens (good and bad) is for your greater good! This mindset shift is where suffering becomes just a part of your life story, causing you to evolve and grow in the process. It becomes something to embrace, as opposed to being the dictator of your very being, impacting your daily life and the decisions and choices you make. Suddenly, your suffering isn't something you hide behind, using it as a shield and reason for not fully living. Instead, it becomes more like a tattoo, worn like a badge of honor. Your suffering becomes a reminder of where you've been and how far you've come. When suffering is no longer an excuse but a reason, you know you're healing. If you work on yourself in order to heal your wounds, the world around you changes for the better.

Out of the Darkness

When my husband first began to pursue a relationship with me, I thought to myself, "Why would this amazing guy want *me*?" At that point in my life, I viewed myself as damaged goods, as having this baggage I was dragging around. I did not believe I deserved him. Even though I prayed to God (despite not practicing any faith for many years up to that point) to bring someone into my life that HE knew was exactly what I needed (and my prayers were answered), I still tried to push him away. Fortunately for me, my husband was relentless in his pursuit. Eventually, I gave in to the idea that just maybe, I didn't know God's plan and I needed to let go of trying to control the outcome.

Suffering had done a number on me up to the time my husband and I got together. I did not love myself. I became an expert at goodbyes and fell way from the moral compass I thought I had. I didn't value the people in my life as I should have and, more importantly, I didn't appreciate myself and my abilities to contribute to the world. When you're lost, you're lost—in every aspect of life. Certainly, it affected my relationships. As I type this, I think back to those years and I don't recognize who that person was.

Did suffering change me? Absolutely. And when I finally dealt with my pain head on, it changed me again—this time for the better. I can say now, with every ounce of my heart, that I am the best version of myself right now. And it was all those challenging moments in my life—the suffering, the grief, marriage, military experience, motherhood, entrepreneurship, life changes, and everything in-between— that allowed me to evolve and grow.

Personal development of myself became my life's mission. Ever since my mid-life crisis in 2014, when I didn't know what else to do, when I was feeling lost or feeling I was failing at motherhood, or was missing purpose, I've sought out ways to grow. This is how suffering has changed me. It's helped me to be able to recognize my emotional pain. I am more equipped now to cope, manage, and shift it into being something useful; a learning tool, if you will, to better myself. I will go deeper into this subject in part three, but for right now, know that you have every ability within you (right now) to make the change you desire.

The cost of not allowing yourself to grow and evolve from suffering is that you become a bitter person, walking around with a chip on your shoulder and feeling as though somehow the world owes you something *because* of your suffering. I know individuals who have suffered greatly in their lives, who carry a sense of entitlement with them wherever they go. They also have a pessimistic black cloud that seems to shift the energy in every room they enter. Interestingly, to them, they're not the bitter, entitled one—everyone else is. There was a time when my relationships with these individuals would carry a lot of tension and friction. We simply did not get along. I realize now it's because we were one and the same. None of us had dealt with our suffering head-on.

It wasn't until I started to make a shift in my own life that I was able to look at those still deep in the midst of their suffering, this time with more understanding, compassion, and empathy. I recognized, deep in my heart, that their pain continued to burn strong and I knew it didn't have to be that way. It saddens me greatly thinking about it. I've been there. I know what that feels like. And I also know what the other side of grief looks and feels like as well.

So imagine if none of us who have suffered grew from our suffering. Is it possible that not healing from pain and suffering and grief could be at the very heart of the turmoil in our world today? That personal pain could be the very thing that is breaking up homes, ending relationships, damaging bonds between parent and child, and forever changing the future generation? It's a deep thought but one I encourage you to ponder, especially if you're suffering right now with grief or emotional pain of any kind.

My relationship with my mother suffered greatly because of grief. I recognize grief as the root of it all—now. I didn't then. I grew up with a grief-ridden mother my entire childhood, and although the feelings only well up intermittently now, it affects me to this day. This is apparent to me whenever conversations of the past come up. Understandably, considering my mother has never been able to fully exonerate herself from the emotional trauma of her past.

Grief (and emotional suffering of various kinds) changed my mom. I know this. I was not yet at the age where we could grieve *together*, as we could if this same tragedy occurred now. It is *when* it happened that changed everything in our relationship. With the power of hindsight, I fully believe that. During a time when bonds between mother and daughter should be strengthened, where as a teenager I could have expressed all the things teenage girls hope to share with their mothers, I did not have that experience. This alone has caused me emotional suffering at various points in my life. My mom was unable to be there for me emotionally. Who can blame her? I certainly do not, but I resented her for a time because of it. I was reminded every time I saw the mother-daughter relationship my peers had, wishing I had the same thing for myself.

Who I did have, though, was my sister. She was then and still is the one I typically go to for things you would expect a daughter to talk to their mother about. She is nine years older than me and the person I'm the closest to, other than my husband.

If I can think of one thing that would have made the difference (at the time) and changed the course of my relationship with my mother, it would have been her seeking therapy for herself, as well as for my brother and myself. My sister was about to graduate high school and was getting ready to venture out on her own. However, had we all been able to seek therapy together, life might have been different for all of us. There is no way to know this for sure, but I imagine it would have been for the better.

When you take the time to work through emotional turmoil, how can the outcome of that, the other side of that pain, not be light? When we discover within ourselves that we are stronger *because of the struggle*, we take power away from the pain itself and the hold it has over us. And *that* is a powerful transformation of pain—from darkness to light.

8

The Blame Game

"Life changing repentance begins where blame shifting ends."

- Timothy Keller

Warning: this chapter, and maybe even the title alone, may cause some defensiveness and jadedness. I am devoting an entire chapter to this because I feel it's that important. It completely ties in with the victimization of grief.

When we feel wronged, the first thing we tend to do is point fingers—in every other direction but our own. How painful it is to admit, to ourselves and to others, that we got it wrong, right? No one likes to surrender; that's just showing weakness, right? Wrong. I dislike being wrong as much as the next person, but I've also learned that the way others perceive you can change when you admit that you were wrong. And not just admit you were wrong but explain how you were wrong. Doing so shows that you take complete ownership and that you fully understand what you bring to the relationship.

Communication is a two-way street. Would you rather be wrong and hated (dragging your own reputation through the mud) or wrong and genuinely liked because you are able to take the high road and admit wrongdoing?

Being an entrepreneur, you get it wrong…*a lot*. Fortunately, this experience alone taught me how to take the high road and eventually how to love myself, ironically enough. Time and again I've had to steer my thoughts away from the path that would make me feel like a victim. No one did that *to* me. More times than I can count, no matter how right I *thought* I was initially, it often turned out that I wasn't.

We can be so sure of something at times that we will fight someone else with words or maybe even our fists, just to make the other surrender. And what is missing in the equation altogether? Self-love. When we approach our communication with others from a place of self-love, there is no judgment and no self-talk stories in the back of our minds influencing us.

What happens, then, when the other person doesn't surrender, and no progress is made? Well then, we blame. We blame the other for the "pain" they inflicted on us: stress, frustration, physical tension or a headache. Our bodies know what our minds are thinking and respond accordingly. This is evident in the body language of others, and it's evident when we feel stress and tension within our own bodies. The body doesn't lie, but the mind does. It's influenced by years and years of stories we keep locked away; the ones we've been fed since childhood and the "truths" we've conjured up over time. By "truths," I mean the ideas, thoughts, and preconceived notions ingrained within us.

The Emotional Cost of Blame

Blame serves no one. Furthermore, it hurts us, our relationships, and our overall well-being. I recall when things didn't go right in my past and although I am generally a flexible, easygoing, go-with-the-flow type of person, I would be triggered and really become the complete opposite: frustrated, angry, and listening to respond not *listening to understand*. I regret those times because often, they were encounters with my children and it was caused by stress from running my business that had nothing to do with them but everything to do with me. When I was feeling like a "victim" in my business, I took it out on those closest to me. You tell me who the real victim was in these situations.

Victimization of grief or emotional suffering of any kind robs us of joy in every aspect of our lives. It becomes a downward spiral, affecting our closest relationships. When you feel like a victim, you want someone to blame—it's a natural and immediate response. I used my entrepreneurial experience as a less serious example, but when it comes to even deeper emotional suffering or grief due to the death of a loved one, the blame can hit us even more deeply where it counts—our own spirituality.

As I mentioned before, I blamed God for a long time. I would not set foot in a church for years unless it was for a wedding. When a long-term relationship ended, I blamed not myself, of course, but my ex. However, when there is no one else to blame but ourselves, because no one else is in the equation, it's just as damaging. Unless we change our attitude, blame—of others or ourselves—solidifies everything we've told ourselves in our minds for years and years. It's as if we fulfill our own ideas about ourselves. We become our own worst critic. I can attest to this as well—maybe even more so when I had my business. Even now as I write these pages, self-doubt creeps up—I simply have to acknowledge it, understand that every author goes through this, and let it go.

Personal Responsibility

So how do we avoid the blame game? I think it is something we first have to learn to recognize and acknowledge. We need to take a bird's-eye view of situations, assess ourselves and our role, find proof of what we believe to be true, and only question ourselves. Could I have gotten this wrong? What story am I telling myself that leads me to believe that the other person is to blame? I love this quote from Robert Anthony: "When you blame others, you give up your power to change."

This is why I am such a huge proponent of personal development in general. We are better able to identify when we're neglecting our own personal responsibility in situations. Personal growth benefits us when we've experienced grief and when we've experienced the end of relationships; in every aspect of our lives it develops our character and changes us...for the better. No matter what has occurred in our lives, when we've taken the time to work on ourselves, we are better able to approach every situation with a new perspective.

I'd wager that you can identify someone you know who lives their life in this manner—or maybe it's even you. This was me at a time when I felt the most lost.

Our minds hold so much power and by not consciously pausing and pondering our thoughts, we give way to *instinctive* thought, which leads to impulsive action, which then leads to self-judgment and—you guessed it—blame, of others or ourselves. We can remove that immediate judgment and the story we tell ourselves and work on changing it over time. Thoughts are just thoughts, and they can be changed—*by our own will and of our own choosing.* Free will…we all have it. Therefore, we can all choose a more positive, win/win approach to people, situations, and life.

Brene Brown, author, doctorate of social work, public speaker, and research professor at the University of Houston, TX stated in her 2013 Ted Talk regarding vulnerability that blame is a way to discharge pain and discomfort, and as a result, we do our best to portray ourselves as perfect. We also pretend that what we do doesn't impact others. Brown goes on to say, in not so many words, that the way we get away from this is to allow our innermost selves to be fully seen. To love with our whole hearts, despite there not being any guarantee. To practice gratitude—leaning into joy and fully believing that you are enough.

Mostly, we blame because there is a part of ourselves that hurts. We are unable to see that which is within ourselves, holding us back from having the joy in our lives we seek. As long as we are stuck in blame, we are stuck in a negative

THE BLAME GAME

mindset and are equally unable to be vulnerable in ways that release us from our pain and suffering.

Grace and Self-Love

Once you can recognize and acknowledge when you are beginning to blame, and have taken inventory of the very thoughts you wish to change, know that being kind to yourself is one of the greatest gifts you can give to yourself. We are so hard on ourselves and will find every reason to either make excuses (if we have yet to acknowledge our personal responsibility) or stay in victim mindset.

A little trick I learned when I was doing my own self-work was to view myself as the child I once was. We are less likely to say out loud to our children or our imaginary child-selves all the hurtful things we actually say to ourselves in our minds. If we would not tell a child they are stupid, fat, incapable, etc., then why on earth do we say these things to ourselves in the quiet of our minds?

Resist the urge to entertain these thoughts. When you find your mind starting to conjure up negative self-talk—pause, acknowledge it, and tell yourself that these things are untrue and why. Then, gracefully and lovingly let it go. I bet I know what you're thinking… "You have got to be kidding! It's not that easy!" I will add that yes, there are times when self-work isn't enough, and we need to enlist the help of medical professionals, but what I will say is the ideas shared in this book *have* worked for me.

You must be a willing participant in your own life and be open-minded and fed up enough to want change. It takes a willingness to admit when you're wrong. It takes tenacity to continue the march to personal well-being, even when the work gets time-consuming, difficult, or emotionally draining.

Giving yourself grace and practicing self-love is a process. You did not neglect your emotional well-being overnight, and you will not recover from it fully overnight either. Take time for you, in whatever way you need—rise early to journal, slowly introduce things into your life that bring you joy, say "no" to the things that drain you and take away from your happiness. Practicing gratitude, as Brene Brown shared, is also important in gaining perspective and appreciation for what is *right* in your world. It is impossible to be angry when you are grateful. Sometimes, a simple mind check of what you're grateful for in a stressful, challenging moment can flip your emotional vibration around.

I understand the premise of this book is grief, but I have recognized that unresolved grief became the basis for so much of the long-ignored emotional unrest that affected all areas of my life for decades. There is a direct link, I believe, between that one event that took place in my childhood and the emotional baggage I collected over time. I think it would be interesting to know, in the course of Brown's research, how many of those people she spoke to had experienced a traumatic life experience (particularly a traumatic childhood experience). If this resonates with you, I would love to hear from you.

There are lessons available to us at every turn, with every encounter, and in seemingly mundane daily living. I invite you to take a typical day and recall when and how many times you had a negative thought about yourself, about someone you met—think about the times when you jump to blame on a dime and ask yourself why that is.

Ask yourself deeper questions that will encourage growth. Step back from the situation, reflect, come from a space of grace and self-love and see how it changes not only your thoughts, but your body language, mood, and the very sensations you feel in your body. Your shoulders will drop, your heart rate will slow down, your breathing will sync to your heartbeat, and your face will soften. Physically, you change your body—inside and out. You will begin to notice, as you start to work on yourself, just how easy it is to sense and witness stress, hurt, and anxiety in others. The difference, though, will be that you will have a new sense of appreciation for their pain and be more compassionate and understanding. Why? Because you've been there and know life is far sweeter when lived in a state of grace and self-love.

PART III:

Life Beyond Grief and Emotional Trauma

9

Disrupt and Change the Pattern

> *"We should be blessed if we lived in the present always, and took advantage of every accident that befell us...*
> *We loiter in winter while it is already spring."*

\- Henry David Thoreau

Have you ever gotten stuck on the thought of *what could have been* when a relationship came to an end (through death or other means)?

I expressed this earlier; being caught in the trap of thinking what could have been is enough to bring on more grief and sadness. And the *fear* of what could be, of the future itself, can keep you stuck in the past, continually replaying in your mind all that you have lost.

Fear is entwined and rooted in our very souls. We have been given the instinct of fight or flight to keep us alive since the days of the saber-toothed tiger. Although, today our saber-toothed tigers are sitting in traffic, debt, or anything else that causes ongoing mental stress. In later chapters, I will touch more on how mental stress manifests in our physical bodies. For now, despite not needing that fight or flight on a daily basis as the first inhabitants of this earth did, it is still ingrained in us, and we simply have to learn to manage stress so we don't find ourselves suffering from chronic stress-induced reactions.

According to Dr. Neil F. Neimark, M.D., of The Academy of Stress Mastery, the fight-or-flight response represents a hardwired early warning system designed to alert us to external environment threats that pose a danger to our physical survival. Because survival is the supreme goal, the system is highly sensitive, set to register minute levels of periodic threat. As such, the fight-or-flight response not only warns us of real external danger but also of the mere perception of danger. This understanding gives us two powerful tools for reducing our stress. They are:

1. **Changing our external environment (our reality).** This includes any action we take that helps make our environment safer. Physical safety means getting out of toxic, noisy, or hostile environments. Emotional safety means surrounding ourselves with friends and family who genuinely care for us, learning better communication skills, time management techniques, and getting out of toxic jobs or bad relationships. Spiritual safety means creating a life surrounded with a sense of purpose, a connection to a higher power, and a resolve to release deeply held feelings of shame, worthlessness, and excessive guilt.

2. **Changing our perception of reality.** This includes any technique used to change our mental perspectives, our attitudes, our beliefs, and our emotional reactions to events. Some techniques I've already touched on within the previous chapters that you can do without a therapist include mirror work and affirmations. Of course, there are more scientific and methodical therapies available with the help of medical professionals. What it comes down to is being able to make lemonade when life hands you lemons. It's the ability to mentally flip the script of what we tell ourselves. Change the story, and you begin to influence the outcome.

One of the best ways I've found to turn down my own fight-or-flight response (or ongoing stress) is with physical exercise. When I am physically active in my life, everything else feels more manageable. When I have allowed myself to be consumed by stress, worry, and self-sabotage, which are all rooted in fear, it was in direct correlation to me not making my well-being a priority.

Fear and Acceptance

I have come to believe that most emotions can be linked back to fear. We react to life out of fear, which causes stress, worry, and self-sabotage. Life would flow more smoothly if we took a proactive approach, learning to fall in sync with the rhythm of life to be in a state of flow. In short, rather than waiting for the shit to hit the fan, we need to listen to our intuition and the signals our body gives us when we're under duress. And consciously (mentally and emotionally) taking a proactive, rather than reactive approach to what life throws our way.

Life isn't meant to be a constant battle. We only make it feel this way if we bombard ourselves with negative thoughts. Grief and emotional trauma come into our lives like a wrecking ball, shattering every belief, mental story, and our very state of being in such a way that we may never recover unless we take back our own power in the situation.

Paying attention to the signals our bodies give us is our first clue that things are starting to go wrong. I can feel the vibe within my own body change when I am in a situation that conjures up stress or sadness. Our physical bodies never lie to us when something isn't right, because our physical bodies react to our mental messages.

Think about this: when you are watching funny animal videos, you may smile or laugh out loud. Do you think your muscles stiffen or your blood pressure rises at that moment? I believe we can all agree that the answer is no. When we feel happy our muscles relax and our blood pressure drops. This is not a stressful fight-or-flight situation, so it makes sense that our bodies react to our physical outside world as well as the inner emotional world. My point being, anything you can do to add more joy to your life will positively impact your overall well-being.

Paying attention to our mind-chatter is one of the first steps in disrupting and changing the patterns. We've become so accustomed to and comfortable with this pattern, we may not even recognize ourselves when we look in the mirror. And I mean *honestly* look at ourselves. Have you ever looked someone in the eyes so deeply that at first, it feels so uncomfortable your only reaction is wanting the moment to end? It can feel that way when we look at ourselves. And if you do any mirror work, this initial experience is typical. It feels silly and unproductive at first. However, after a while, you begin to see yourself not as a physical body but more as a soul and everything that makes you you.

It is a powerful feeling to be able to see yourself as more than just a physical body, walking around, going to work, interacting and reacting to the world around you. To see yourself and the world around you as light energy, and with the understanding that we are all spiritual beings here to have a physical experience—nothing more, nothing less. It's not a matter of having a "rose-colored glasses" approach to life, but rather seeing life itself for what it is—an experience. We are here to experience, not to constantly struggle, react, and mentally beat ourselves up day after day. This idea alone can shift thoughts in an upward direction. Acceptance of what is can be life-changing.

Acceptance, one of the stages of grief recognized by Kubler-Ross, is an important step of moving on from grief and emotional trauma. When you allow yourself to accept what is, you can begin to let go of what was and what will never be. Not that it will cease to be hurtful or emotional, but it's no longer giving those feelings power and making you feel powerless.

Surrendering to Growth

Finally, surrendering to what it is that you cannot change can open you to joy and give you opportunity for growth which you may never have experienced without grief and/or emotional trauma. And that's what I am hoping you can see as you read these pages. I realize emotional suffering doesn't seem like much of a gift at the time it occurs in our lives, but as I sit here right now, typing these words, I can attest that suffering, eventually, can be the very thing that helps you grow.

You can choose, on any given day, if you want to use the events or circumstances you endure in your life as a learning tool or a very long self-detached vacation. What I mean when I say that is, when we choose not to get in touch with our inner selves and address the very things that cause friction in our lives, we're choosing pain and suffering. We decide to vacate the real parts of ourselves that can teach us the most and change us in a positive way. But that path to growth is painful, and we tend to choose the path of least resistance. That is what so much of our lives become when we endure suffering of any kind: a game of cat and mouse with our own inner "demons."

These "demons" are all those things that bring us discomfort to think about, let alone talk about. They are the skeletons in our emotional closets that, when triggered, abruptly arise from the shadows of our souls so that we become someone we no longer recognize, in the most trivial of circumstances. Isn't it a wonder, then, why sometimes you can have an encounter with someone, and you walk away and just think to yourself, "Wow, that person is a real jerk!"

We all have moments where *we* are that person and encounter individuals who seem to be having a bad day. However, when you are continually hiding from your own shadow, it's not just a bad day, it's a bad week, a bad year, or worse, a negative existence. It manifests in every single area of our lives.

Things came to a head for me when I was experiencing inner angst around whether to close my photography studio or not. I created this monster of emotional anxiety, which to me felt like a mid-life crisis. I was lost—yet again. And that's the thing about our shadows. They tend to follow in our footsteps. And until we shine a light on our shadows, they will remain and come with us throughout life. No matter how much I thought I had things under control and thought I was living my life based on my values and morals up to that point, there was always this nagging feeling of not doing or being enough. The more I tried to compensate and show up for others, the less I showed up for myself, and the bigger my shadow grew. Also, the more confused I became, until I finally started asking myself better questions. And asking and asking until I got to the root of it all: fear.

We fear acceptance itself, on some level. As soon as we accept, the sooner we acknowledge. Once there's acknowledgment, we're then forced to confront what we need to change.

Flipping the Mindset Switch

Although adaptability is my greatest strength and I am not easily flustered by change, it's a bit different when we must face the change within ourselves that needs to take place. It's far easier to rearrange our lives than it is to change ourselves because, and I believe we all tell ourselves this from time to time, it's not us that needs to change, right? It's the other person; the difficult one, the rebellious one, the negative Nancy that needs to change, right? Ah, I know. That possibly feels good to read, thinking you're getting some validation. But, what I will tell you is that sometimes it is ourselves that need to change. We give permission to everyone and everything that is in our lives. Could it be, then, that those people and things are mirrors of ourselves, reflecting back to us what needs to change within us?

This idea was not an easy concept for me to get behind when I first started to read about it while working on my own personal development. I do believe people or situations are brought into our lives to teach us something. There's a lesson we need to learn, and we ask for it by our very state of being. For example, I think we all know someone that, no matter how much advice you give them, never listens. Their life just seems to be one challenge after another. Now, imagine that same person completely changes their outlook on life, flips their mindset from negative to positive, and does some soul-searching personal growth work. They would carry themselves differently and the universe would probably respond to them differently. I'm not saying that bad things don't happen to good people—not at all. What I am saying is this: our own mindset and outlook has everything to do with how we respond to situations and how strongly those situations affect us. I believe there's a reason some people live longer than others and it has a lot to do with mindset.

It comes back to us being spiritual souls here to have a human experience. What better way to grow spiritually than to have a mirror held to us at every turn in life?

All of this may sound a little woo-woo to you, and I fully accept that. I also know that some or all of it may make sense to some. It honestly depends on where you are in your life. When I first started working on myself, I would shut down at the first mention of such things, because to me, it was all a little too woo-woo. As I started to write and do affirmation work, as well as look at the bigger picture and the long term (which is really hard for me because I have a more moment-by-moment personality), I realized my future did not look too bright if I were to keep on the way I was.

When I began to visualize and connect with the feelings I wanted to feel on a daily basis, I discovered what I wanted to contribute to the world (again, through writing and self-work). I started to see a lost aspect of myself reemerge. I began to feel lighter, more joyful and inspired. I began to discover a newfound purpose for life. That thought alone excited me. So much felt possible when I embraced that joy and inspiration. So, I committed myself to the process of my personal growth, and I haven't looked back. It has completely changed my life.

I believe anyone can be their own hero. You must, however, commit to the process, through thick and through thin, and never give up on yourself. It's the old stories on repeat in your mind that are trapping you. It's the thoughts that chain your better self to your past hurt, emotional trauma, shame, and constant fear. That is the real shame, because you suffer unnecessarily, as does everyone in your life.

10

Make a Choice, to Take the Chance, to Make a Change

"I know of no more encouraging fact than the unquestionable ability of man to elevate his life by a conscious endeavor."

- Henry David Thoreau

Life: it's a series of choices. Options are thrown at us left and right on a daily basis. All of us are faced with decisions that need to be made; many of them are minor and don't affect our lives much, however, some decisions may feel like an enormous burden.

If you are a parent, your day is full of decisions. From the child's perspective, the world is full of options, so much so, it may feel overwhelming. There are many moments in my adult life where I feel like that overwhelmed child with too many options. From a young age, and still to this day, I do not like too many options and have developed my own way of making decisions when the plethora of choices outweighs my ability to make a decision.

For example, nowadays as an adult, when I am in the grocery store, and I'm picking up something I don't usually buy, I will look at which brand or flavor there is the least of left. I tell myself, "It must be good if there's hardly any left." This is the logic I go with when I'm unsure, and I can truthfully say it has served me well on most occasions.

Overall, I tend to be a creature of habit and don't typically stray from everyday purchases in the grocery store. When shopping otherwise, I rely heavily on shared reviews and will do my research for almost everything I buy. I think this method of decision-making was greatly influenced by my childhood and way of growing up, just like so much of us is affected by our childhoods.

Inner Chaos Equals Outer Chaos

Growing up, there wasn't an abundance of anything. I grew up in a modest home, nothing fancy. Inside there wasn't an abundance of material things. It is this simplistic approach to living that, to this day, is apparent in my life.

Today, I have more furniture than we did back then, but everything has its place. When clutter begins to accumulate, it causes me stress. It's interesting because my siblings live the same way; everything has its place, and there's no clutter. But, we all have rooms or spaces where we unleash our clutter, don't we? The spaces not everyone can see at first glance. Just as we have clutter within areas of our minds and hearts.

If you've ever seen shows where there are stories about people who hoard things and live in filthy conditions, the idea is that there is so much internal chaos that it gets expressed in their outside world. I believe this to be true. I've seen similar things myself, and it usually indicated that the person is going through internal turmoil.

Rather than cram our spaces with clutter and stuff and allow it to get out of control, we do everything we can to control the chaos. And we do this with our own minds as well. We exhaust ourselves trying to control our natural tendencies and *not* be our authentic selves. And we do this because it ties into all the previous chapters: we have lost who we truly are due to emotional trauma. Shame, fear, lack of personal responsibility for what we bring into our lives, and victim mindset, etc.

Doesn't it make sense then, that when you've experienced emotional trauma, it manifests in all areas of your life? How it does will greatly vary from person to person. It all depends on what stage of life the emotional trauma took place, and also the person's current mindset. By the time we reach adulthood, we've already formed the stories and personal bias in our minds. So when emotional trauma or grief takes place first as an adult, it can either be the one thing that completely shatters your world, or it could be the very thing that brings you the spiritual awareness you may have never experienced otherwise and changes you for the better.

As a child, I believe you have little power or choice in how you respond to grief or emotional suffering. Cognitively, there is a lot of mental development taking place and children, in general, approach life very differently than adults. Children live in the moment and still have that natural wonder and curiosity about the world.

I'm no expert on child development, but I think we can all agree that children are a clean slate and it's the adult world and society that writes on the slate of who children become. For me personally, I think not having the cognitive ability to choose to have the victim mindset as a child protected me in a way. When I was around ten years old and was the caretaker of the home and the emotional caretaker of my mother, I grew up fast, but I don't recall seeing myself as a victim. I just thought these were things everyone my age did. I didn't know any different. It wasn't until my later teen years, when I started to mentally and emotionally mature, that my "rose-colored glasses" approach to life began to shift.

Up until about two years ago, I greatly struggled with decision-making. I would analyze the crap out of everything. I would turn situations every which way, thinking about pros and cons, and make ridiculous lists. I would stress myself out to the point it would affect my health. I simply did not want to make the wrong choice and live with regret. That was at the core of every difficult decision I had to make. I was fearful, and I did not trust my own intuition. This was my mindset around decision-making most of my adult life. It's what caused me to seek counsel from too many people, which only added to my stress and anxiety about making a decision, because I then had even more opinions to think through. I simply could not look ahead to the future. I was incapable of seeing the big picture and was so stuck in the present.

In a lot of ways, I am still that child who, like all children, lives in the moment. I also still have a difficult time looking ahead to the future, to create goals and plan my days based on the things I wish to accomplish. Today, I need a kick in the pants and accountability to see my big goals come to fruition. In fact, a beta group on writing a book in ninety days is the only reason I'm writing these words right now. It's all about accountability and the big picture; the very things I struggle with, as well as trusting myself and the process. If you're like me and struggle with decision-making, you likely also struggle with trusting yourself. I often find myself looking elsewhere for validation. This is something I still work on. Having the experiences I've had and being open to challenges has definitely helped in that regard.

The Gift of Intuition

Making choices today has definitely gotten easier, because I've learned to trust myself and my intuition. I started to listen more to my internal voice, and so far, so good. It's really how I found the book-writing beta program in the first place. One thing has to lead to the next thing. Tuning out the world, getting still, and releasing all judgment (basically, meditation) is all about separating the mind from the heart. I never understood what my problem was until I realized this. I just was not separating the two. My feelings and my thoughts tend to commingle, which then doesn't allow my intuition to surface. When I quiet myself, when I journal, or when I tune out the world, this is when my magic happens.

Your magic may come to you in different ways. Maybe it's exercise that stimulates your heart and allows your mind to be free during that time. Or maybe it's on a nature walk (which I personally enjoy as well) or in a bubble bath. Whatever is easiest for you to give your mind rest so your heart can speak to you (your inner voice and intuition) is where you'll find your magic. Once you find what that is, do more of it. The answers to all the decisions you are faced with are there.

Instead we have the tendency to convolute our minds with not only our personal biases, stories, and opinions, but also those of others. Why? Because we ask them. And even when we don't ask, we *assume* we know what they're thinking. Really, it's none of our business what other people think about us in their own minds. The thoughts of others are theirs and theirs alone to own. We can only control our own thoughts. Again, it goes back to thoughts becoming things, and our thoughts greatly influence our decisions and our ability to make those decisions.

Until you decide to make a choice, to take the chance, to make a change, absolutely nothing changes. Once you make a choice, you've taken the chance, and that's half the battle right there. From the simplest of decisions, you have to accept the outcome. And maybe this is where people don't move forward in tough life decisions; there's a certain expectation we attach to our decisions.

Let's say, for instance, you make the decision to quit your job and relocate. You will likely have some sort of expectation of how that will all go. You expect it will be a stressful transition, which is reasonable. What you don't expect is that, although you love the *idea* of rural living, it turns out you hate the lack of convenience and all the things that come with small-town life. What you didn't expect is that your children will love it and maybe your spouse. Then what? Either you meet and compromise and make another change, uprooting your family yet again, or accept the outcome (hopefully without resentment or frustration towards your spouse and/or family).

Once you *choose* to marry and once you *decide* to bring children into your marriage, you've decided your life is no longer just about you. So everything you've experience in your life, your ability (or inability) to listen to your intuition, to quiet your mind, and to really *own* the choices you make, becomes more important than ever. It's a disservice not only to ourselves but to those we love when we neglect our intuition.

Intuition, by definition, is the ability to understand something immediately, without the need for conscious reasoning. Also, it is a thing that one knows or considers likely from instinctive feeling rather than conscious reasoning; the power or faculty of attaining direct knowledge or cognition without evident rational thought or inference.

What a beautiful gift that has been given to us, at our disposal whenever we need it. Humor me and read the definition above again. There is a mighty power within your soul. You need not seek the advice or guidance of others when all that you will ever need to know is within you. Granted, I realize it may be necessary to seek professional help in order to even get to this point in your life. I am speaking to those whose hearts and minds are open to the power of their own intuition right now. It does take time to get there.

By deciding *you* are reason enough to choose a more joyful way of living, you're already choosing joy. Only good things can come from taking care of your own mental, physical, and spiritual well-being. Invest in yourself, and you invest in everyone and everything you bring into your life. Choosing is half the battle. Even though it is challenging work to improve upon ourselves, making the conscious and intuitive choice every day to choose how you want to feel will cause more expansion in your life than you ever imagined. I'm living proof as I'm writing these words I've only before *dreamed* of writing.

11

Mind Is Everything

*"All that we are is the result of what we have
thought.
The mind is everything.
What we think, we become."*

- The Buddha

This is probably one of my favorite chapters and topics on the matter of changing our lives for the better; on moving beyond grief and emotional suffering. It's that old saying of "mind over matter." The phrase first appeared in 1863 in *The Geological Evidence of the Antiquity of Man* by Sir Charles Lyell. It was first used to refer to the increasing status and evolutionary growth of the minds of animals and man throughout Earth history. The phrase also relates to the ability to control the perception of pain that one may or may not be experiencing. The original statement, in its use by Lyell in 1863, is as follows:

"It may be said that, so far from having a materialistic tendency, the supposed introduction into the earth at successive geological periods of life—sensation, instinct, and intelligence of the higher mammalian bordering on reason, and lastly, the improbable reason of Man himself—presents us with a picture of the ever-increasing dominion of mind over matter."

The Mind-Body Connection

This idea comes back to where I mentioned the mind-body connection and how our thoughts become things and affect our physical bodies as a result. Pro athletes, special military forces, even Buddhists, have this ability to control their bodies with their minds. Or maybe it's their ability to detach their thoughts from their minds? I find the mind-body connection fascinating and, when studied, it can be a teaching tool for how anyone can find solitude within their minds to "survive." Do we know when our minds are having a fight-or-flight response? No, it's a physiological reaction due to perceived immediate danger—or in our world today, chronic stress.

Walter Bradford Cannon was the person who first described the theory of "fight or flight response" in animals or "acute stress response" in vertebrates and other organisms—a reaction to threat whereby there is a general discharge of the sympathetic nervous system, preparing the animal or organism for fighting or fleeing.

Later, in 1994, "acute stress disorder" was introduced and described as acute traumatic stress in the initial month after trauma that is predictive of PTSD (Post Traumatic Stress Disorder). During that same period, Australian psychiatrist Richard Bryant, whose main areas of interest are PTSD and Prolonged Grief Disorder, established the Traumatic Stress Clinic in Australia.

Prolonged Grief Disorder (PGD), according to Wikipedia, is relatively rare—experienced by about ten percent of bereaved survivors. The affected person is incapacitated by grief, to the point of feeling in constant turmoil, with a continued inability to adjust to daily life without the loved one six months or more after the death. The symptoms of PGD are intense yearning for the person, identity confusion, difficulty accepting the loss, bitterness, emotional numbness, inability to trust others, and the feeling of being trapped in grief.

Known risk factors that separate PGD from Major Depression Disorder, PTSD, and Generalized Anxiety Disorder (GAD), include a history of:

- Childhood separation anxiety
- Controlling parents
- Parental abuse or death
- Close kinship relationship to the deceased (e.g., parents)
- Insecure attachment styles
- Emotional dependency
- Lack of preparation for death
- Death in hospital

PGD symptoms have been associated with:

- Increase in suicidal thoughts or suicide
- Cancer
- Immunity dysfunction
- High blood pressure
- Cardiac events
- Motor impairment
- Risky health behaviors
- Reduced quality of life in adults and in children
- Increased use of medical services or loss of work

PGD requires targeted treatment consisting of psychotherapy designed specifically for PGD. Preliminary results of an online self-management intervention to prevent PD in recently bereaved individuals, in a study called "HEAL" (Healthy Experiences After Loss), are very promising. Currently, there is a larger randomized controlled trial being planned.

Up until the time of writing, I had not heard of PGD. What comes to mind reading about it is this: considering this is still a relatively newly named disorder, I can only imagine the magnitude of its reach. It's important to be able to recognize there are varying degrees of grief, which brings me to a whole new can of worms: typically normal grief vs. unhealthy grief.

People die every single day. Death is a part of life. We all know this. But how can we ensure we don't become a statistic of grief? How do we differentiate and recognize when our emotional pain has reached a point where there needs to be an intervention with treatment?

Today, we don't just have grief to deal with but all of the pressures of life. This is why I write so passionately about personal growth from emotional pain and personal growth in general. Life is not meant to be easy. How else would we learn, grow, evolve, and adapt if not for the struggles life hands us?

Fortunately, prolonged turmoil, as is described with PGD, is not typical. And fortunately, for the majority, moving on from grief *is* possible. As I've mentioned before, I believe grief never leaves but rather comes and goes throughout one's life in waves.

We've become somewhat desensitized to grief by our own means of doing what we can to evade, numb, or distract ourselves from it. This is where grief begins to be unhealthy. We are much better off when we can recognize when we need an emotional time out. Doing so gives ourselves the permission (and the time) to sit with the feelings, fully processing what it is we're feeling.

Processing feelings of grief and emotional trauma is going to be different for everyone. Just as we are all unique in who we are, so are our grieving and emotional trauma experiences. I'm not going to pretend to know how you should grieve or tell you what you need to do to get beyond your grief, as I do not have intimate details of your story. By using my story, however, maybe you can relate. Hopefully, by sharing what has worked for me and what I've learned in my own grieving process, you glean some information you find beneficial in your own healing.

Intention, Purpose, and Conscious Living

When I first started taking a long, hard look inward, I found myself drawn to people, books, programs, etc. that were in the genre of personal development. One author would lead me to another, one book would lead me to a blog, one social media influencer would lead me to the next, and so on. It became this snowball of information coming at me, teaching me various ways of getting beyond the blocks I'd been dealing with in my life.

Also, during this time, I found myself really struggling with my relationships. I was in this limbo stage of not feeling comfortable in my own skin. I recognized all the ways I had sabotaged myself, and, as a result, my relationships. I was so beside myself I convinced my husband I needed a dog. Truthfully—that is not a joke.

Our youngest was just about to start kindergarten, and I would find myself alone (all day) five days a week. Based on the emotional rollercoaster I was already on, I knew having that kind of "freedom" would drive me stir-crazy. I write "freedom" intentionally with quotations because, to me, I was already in my own emotional prison. Having idle time, although I knew it would give me time to work on myself, only meant there were no more excuses. I could no longer evade the thoughts that had been consuming me. I would be alone with those thoughts and feelings. I was scared of what it would all mean—would *I* have to change?

So, I set out to find a dog; my way to distract myself from myself. I researched breeds, settling on a Havanese. And lo and behold, I found a Havanese breeder less than six hours from me who would be willing to meet halfway. My husband reluctantly agreed (he is not one for animals in the home) because I convinced him a dog was what *I* needed and that, although we've tried twice before to have rescue dogs, this time would be different. I would raise this dog to be just as I groomed him to be: trained to be respectful of our home, to be a great companion for our family, and an overall successful "pet project" for me—literally.

Before I brought Gizmo (three years old at the time of writing) home, I read up on how to choose and train a puppy. Choosing the right puppy, to me, was the most crucial step and one that proved to be the most important in selecting the perfect pup for my family. Three years later, he has been the perfect dog. I take a lot of pride in the pooch he's become. When I look at him, I see a lot more than just a dog I trained well. I see a creature that truly helped me through a tough time. As cliché as that may sound, Gizmo, along with the self-work I was doing in conjunction with his training, was the best therapy for me at that time.

What gets me when I think about it is this: I had never even heard of a Havanese. I had never desired to have a puppy or to mess with all the training that goes into raising a puppy (hence, previously going with rescue dogs). And what are the chances there would be a breeder within driving distance of a breed not very commonly known? Yes, I researched, but honestly, I believe this is where thoughts become things. This idea has been proven to me many times over since I started living with more personal awareness.

There isn't much I do these days without intention and purpose. I choose, daily, to bring everything into my life from a conscious level. Yes, there are days I feel the complete opposite. The difference is, though, now I am able to recognize it. I am better equipped and able to sense when things are going in the wrong direction within my mind or body, and it's directly related to when I start getting passive in my self-awareness work. I start to feel aches and pains, my mind starts entertaining more negative thinking, and I just feel out of flow with life.

I believe I've made it clear that this hasn't been an easy place to get to in my life. But anyone, and I mean anyone, can do it. I firmly and truly believe that. Yes, it may require additional professional therapy, as I understand some people simply cannot do it on their own as I have these past two years. Previously, however, I too sought help outside of myself. What I needed the most, however, was to get clear and transparent with myself. No one else could do that or facilitate that for me. I simply used and sought out tools to help me along the way.

In previous chapters, I've described some of the tools I've used. If you go to my website, www.theguidedheart.com, you may subscribe to receive a printable PDF of resources I recommend, as well as new blog posts to your inbox. Also, I have a "Resources" page, where I include every resource I've personally incorporated into my self-work process. I also offer insight into how each resource has helped me.

12

Create a Road Map and Take Action

"Let's not forget that the little emotions are the great captains of our lives, and we obey them without realizing it."

- Vincent Van Gogh

You've made a choice to take a chance to make a change—to move beyond your grief and/or emotional suffering. Now what? It's not as simple as just one day waking up and deciding you'll let intuition be your guide. I wish it were. I wish it had been for me. Wow, it would've saved me a lot of self-torment and years of heartache had it been that simple!

Like a muscle, intuition needs to be flexed and strengthened from the ground up. It is within all of us, but if we don't work on our bare bones, we'll never even trust our intuition for what it is. We'll continue to second-guess, seek advice and validation from others, and remain stuck on the hamster wheel. You'll feel as though you're spinning your wheels and getting nowhere, which is *not* a fun, adventurous, and joyful way to go about this one life we're given.

Creating a road map for your life requires big-picture thinking. As I previously mentioned, I often struggle with this. I tend to focus on the here and now and what I need to do today. Although I don't easily stress over things that don't get done today that can be done tomorrow, I do get stressed when I feel like I'm not moving in an upward direction and all of my effort is getting me nowhere.

What happens when we put undue pressure on ourselves or when we have certain expectations of an outcome that aren't being met? We give up. I've given up on plenty of things. Actually, my life appears to be a series of stops and starts. I gain momentum, but as soon as I feel like I'm losing momentum and am not making progress, I give up. Eventually, I begin again, but it's twice as hard to start over.

What I never gave up on, though, was figuring this out about myself. I never gave up on trying to better understand who I am and why I do what I do and sit through the emotional pain that came with doing that.

What I believe catapulted this desire for me to figure myself out and make the necessary changes within myself was reflecting on every birthday I've had since turning thirty-five years old and experiencing a mid-life crisis as a result. I've had this ticking clock in the back of my mind with every passing year, reminding me that I'm approaching forty years old. To me, assuming I live into my eighties (which to me is a good, long life and the average lifespan), my life is nearly half over. As doomsday as it sounds, these thoughts alone have made me decide, once and for all, to pursue individual endeavors now, as opposed to someday.

I'm not sure if this is something a lot of women talk about. I think a mid-life crisis is viewed as a male experience, which is why I've likely only seen messages through television, radio, and such where it's the male counterpart that is moving on from relationships or buying the sports car he's always wanted. After experiencing it myself, I know I can't be the only one. And maybe our past is what predisposes us to have a mid-life crisis in the first place? I'm not sure. What I am certain of is that the experience shook me to my core and brought up all of my old baggage.

When you desire so strongly to be of service to others but for the love of God can't seem to figure out what that looks like, it's tormenting. That's where I was emotionally towards the end of my photography business. I knew I had more to offer the world. I was providing a fantastic service and product to my clients; however, I wasn't feeling "juiced up" in my life. I was desiring more. I just didn't know what that was or what "more" looked like.

Resistance

I resisted and protested this feeling for an entire year, worked on myself in the process, and out of that I found the clarity I was looking for. The resistance was my mid-life crisis. I was not open to possibility, I was unable to look into the future, and I wasn't feeling that everything in my life was for my greater good. This was the most difficult thing for me to grasp. I needed to surrender my cares, worries, and frustrations to God and the powers of being and accept my situation and life for what it is. This became my mantra: it is what it is; let it go.

Ultimately, everything we do in our lives is driven by our need to avoid pain and our desire to gain pleasure. We will do far more, however, to prevent pain than we will to gain pleasure. This is where we tend to procrastinate, of which I am often guilty. I have discovered I procrastinate because I am focusing on the wrong thoughts. When we aren't focused on how *not* changing our behavior will be even more painful than changing it and how actually *changing it* will bring measurable and immediate pleasure, we procrastinate. It's really the reason it's taken me two years to write this book. I was focused on the details and the painful process of having to figure it all out rather than the pain I would feel at never doing it.

Ask yourself: "When I'm sitting in my rocking chair when I'm eighty years old, what will I regret having never done?" Likewise, when you're faced with a problem, ask yourself: "Five months from now, will this still matter?" Better questions, inevitably, lead to better answers.

When grief or emotional trauma has reached beyond a point where you can carry on with life in a positive way, it's imperative to find a purpose in order to get things back on track. Not doing so will only lead to more emotional pain in the future. The thought of a future of more pain should be motivation enough to shift your life in a positive direction. What do you really want out of life? I imagine you want to experience more joy. Reasons for wanting it come first. Once you know you want it and why, how to go about getting it comes next.

The process of getting out of the grips of emotional pain and all the baggage that goes along with it will be different for everyone. I'm not suggesting what I say is a one-approach-fits-all. Rather, take bits and pieces that feel right to you. Do the things you feel you can commit to for the long-term. Personal growth of any kind is a long-term commitment. By committing daily to learning more about yourself, you will unlock potential for yourself and your life you never knew existed. But first, you must believe it's possible.

My Approach to Personal Growth

Below, I will outline the step-by-step process I used when I started my personal growth journey. The majority of these I did simultaneously, but I truly had the time to spend on them. Sometimes, when we fall flat on our faces and hit rock bottom, it just so happens free time is a byproduct of that. I can see now that this was and is a blessing in disguise. So, if this is you, consider it a blessing. It just might be the motivation you need to make *you* a priority.

What I wouldn't recommend, and what my personal growth looked like in the beginning, was me in my pj's nearly all day long. I would skip meals, live on coffee, and bury myself in self-help books, programs, and blogs. I poured every fiber of my being into getting my shit together and creating a different future for myself. All the while, my emotional wreckage was showing on the outside. It was an ugly process. And really, your personal growth doesn't have to go this way.

Here are five things, in no particular order, to get you on a good start to personal growth.

• **Paper and a Writing Tool:** Get a notebook or a journal you love the feel of or that gives you the feeling of joy looking at it. After you've worked through significant emotional hurdles (and need less actual writing space), you can move to a bullet-type journal or a journal with prompts. I have always used a traditional lined journal. My current one zips, has a ribbon bookmark, and has a Bible passage embossed on the cover. I also use Danielle LaPorte's Weekly Planner, which I love and is a great complement to my regular journaling. She also offers a Daily Planner version. My writing tool of choice is Uni-ball's jetstream in fine point blue. Use what you love, and you'll love using it.

Journaling through your feelings allows you to release and work through them, which, in turn, will help you to find solutions. Begin by asking a question at the start of your entry. Write whatever shows up; let the thoughts flow. You will be amazed at what you discover and realize on your own. Go back and reference the writing prompt mentioned in chapter one.

You may find you need quiet to write. Having space without distractions might be your thing, too. While others may like the chatter and sounds of a coffee house in the background, I personally like it quiet. When I'm writing for other purposes, I do like to have various "focus" or "concentration" mixes on Spotify playing in the background. Create the environment you need to concentrate on getting your thoughts on paper.

Also, your mission in journaling shouldn't be about finding blame in others for your situation. The purpose is to find within yourself why you feel the way you feel; to discover and use the power and control you have over yourself to change the narrative. Writing is a powerful tool that far too few utilize or take the time to do, and it pays back in dividends. It does not have to take a lot of time either. Focus on one question per day, set a timer (if you need to), and purge the thoughts that create mental chatter.

• **Self-Improvement Programs:** In the beginning, when I first decided to start making significant shifts in my life, I came across life coach guru Tony Robbins. I thought to myself if there was anything I could do, I wanted to be doing what he was doing. He has a Netflix documentary called *I Am Not Your Guru*. Check it out, and you'll understand what I mean.

Tony has a way with people. His gift is to take the most depressed people, suicidal even, and immediately change their lives. It is on my bucket list to meet him, for sure. Anyway, I completed his programs, "The Time of Your Life" and "Personal Power." I also got his book, *Money, Master the Game*. It's so thick and chock-full of so much info, I have yet to get through it all. He is such an inspiration to me. I highly recommend anything he puts out into the world.

One of the key takeaways from Tony's teachings (and there are many) is this: stress comes from making things more important than they really are. Everything you experience in your life starts with the thoughts in your own head. We all get our "musts."

Change your "shoulds" to "musts" and settle for nothing less. Tony says, throughout his various teachings, "What's wrong is always available and so is what's right."

Available Resources

There were other programs I went through as well but none like Tony's. My point in sharing this is: there are a lot of resources at our disposal in this day and age. There is no reason why anyone can't work on improving themselves. My question is: what do you have to lose by trying?

Once you can understand and accept where you are, start working backward to start figuring out how you got there. You don't want to carry the same habitual patterns, attitudes, and behaviors into your future, so you need to address them to ditch them. Hopefully, this list aids you in getting off to a good start on your own personal growth journey.

• **Books:** I used to read fiction: thrillers and murder mysteries. Once I started my photography business, though, I quickly learned about all of my shortcomings. This is when I turned to non-fiction: self-improvement and business books. Reading non-fiction has given me so much perspective. It also brought back my love of learning and reading again. Do you have to read non-fiction? No. Will reading non-fiction make you a better person? Not necessarily. But, can one book change your life? Absolutely. Most of the non-fiction I've read is geared towards aspects of entrepreneurship. The following are just some of the books that impacted me the most. I encourage you to do your own search for books that you think may resonate with you personally. These books were either recommended to me, or I've followed the author for a while and knew their book would be beneficial to me.

Financial Advice by Tony Robbins

I highly recommend Tony Robbins' books, for example, his new one, *Unshakeable: Your Financial Freedom Playbook, Creating Peace of Mind in a World of Volatility*. One hundred percent of the proceeds from his previous book (and current book) have gone and are going to an organization Tony is passionate about, Feeding America. This man is my mentor. He's beaten incredible odds in his own life and created an empire simply by helping people, giving back over and over to organizations he cares about in the process.

Discover Your Strengths

It is much easier to utilize your strengths than it is to work on improving or focusing on your weaknesses. *Strengths Finder 2.0* by Tom Rath will help you to figure out what your core strengths are and then provide you with scenarios or ideas in which those strengths may be applied in your life. Today, I know what I am good at and understand that some things are better left to other individuals with a different skill-set. This is especially important if you are an entrepreneur, the leader of any organization, or in any form of employment, no matter what that may be. This book doesn't seem to fit with the others here, but it, as well as other online resources, helped me get into the nitty-gritty of my traits and personality. When we understand ourselves better, we perform better in all areas of our lives. That was my goal with this book and other resources like it.

Another resource I recommend that is not a book, but along the same lines as *Strengths Finder 2.0*, is How to Fascinate by Sally Hogshead. This is an online website where you can take a personality quiz that measures how others perceive you at your best. Learn how to make a better first impression, with your most influential traits. I found it useful and informative, not to mention interesting. She also has a few books out as well.

Spiritual Reading

I have been reading the daily devotional, *Living Faith*, for a few years now. This little soft-cover book comes out quarterly and is provided by my church and can even fit in a small purse. I really do love this little book. It is my daily dose of God's word and is a source of inspiration for me to be the best person I can be. It is a challenge to work on bettering ourselves, given the type of world we live in today, and this book is a pause button on life for me. It is often the source of inspiration for my journal entries and blog posts as well. Whether it be this book or another like it, over time you grow to appreciate its positive effect on you in the moment. If you are interested, *Living Faith* is available on AmazonKindle, Nook, and iBookstore.

If you've fallen away from your faith, this is also an excellent way to slowly introduce yourself back to it again or to deepen your spirituality. In the moment of grace and gratitude, it is impossible to be angry. This is one way I accomplish that. Another suggestion, if you're not a reader, is the Bible app, which is available in iTunes. You can actually have the Bible read to you in 365 days, by listening to little snippets each day. I haven't gotten through an entire year of listening every day, but from time to time I will listen while I'm doing dishes or cleaning. It's another way to put a pause button on the mental chatter in your mind and feed your spirit with something positive and life-enriching.

Another book about spiritual mastery recommended to me by my life coach and friend, Angela Goodeve, is *Happier than God* by Neale Donald Walsch. It is a guidebook on how to create an extraordinary spiritual life. It isn't as much about religion as it is about the soul-spirit. It explains how we manifest our own realities and ways to change those realities; that what you resist persists and what you look at disappears. This is exactly my point here, in my own book: the only way out is through; confront that which you've been ignoring and stuffing down so you can release it. This book is an excellent companion as you work to do that.

Motivational Reading

Think & Grow Rich by Napoleon Hill—I know, the title exudes greed and materialism in a way. I didn't get this book because my goal in life is to be rich. Rather, I wanted to read this book to see what I was doing wrong because I was feeling stuck in life. This book is motivating and inspiring, to say the least. "What the mind can conceive, the mind can achieve," as Hill states, drives home the idea of how much our thought patterns impact our lives. I highly recommend this book, even if you're not an entrepreneur. This book will grow and expand your mind. It's also a great book to keep around to re-read, which I have, or to one day pass on to your kids. It is the limiting beliefs within our minds that keep us from making progress, and those same limiting beliefs are the ones we pass on to the next generation.

Parenting: It's More about You than You Think

The Conscious Parent by Shefali Tsabary, PhD is one of those books I wish I had read when I first became a parent. I only recently read this, actually. I highly recommend this book to parents or legal guardians. As I've said before, self-work is an ongoing process and journey. I don't think it's a destination at which you ever *arrive.* This book brings to light the baggage we carry from one generation to the next. It offers a different perspective, highlighting where, as parents, we all make mistakes, even though we think what we're doing is best. This book will cause self-reflection. If you have a weak relationship with your child, this book may also be just what you need to help you repair that relationship. Because, more often than not, it's not the child that's the problem, it is us—the parent.

Dealing with Emotional Trauma

Loyalty to Your Soul by H. Ronald Hulnick, PhD and Mary R. Hulnick, PhD is another that was recommended by my life coach. It does have "homework," but again, it's a great reference as you work through your emotional trauma. It can be a difficult read, discussing theories and ideas that you may be hearing for the first time (it is written by PhDs), but I encourage you to see it through. If you're open to conscious awakening and changing your life, and would like to see the world through a new lens, I encourage you to give this book a try. It goes along well with the other books mentioned and will be a useful tool as you work through your feelings.

A New Spin on Goal-Setting

I have to warn you, *The Desire Map* by Danielle LaPorte is work. It is all about creating goals that serve your spirit and your soul; creating the life you desire using "how you want to feel" as your guide. I have changed how I make decisions because of this book, giving more thought to how I want to feel, as opposed to basing my actions on the expectations of others. This book puts a whole new spin on decision-making. Again, highly recommended as you start to shape a life you desire. You can say no gracefully to the things that no longer serve you in your life. And you will start to say yes and incorporate more things that bring joy into your life if you commit to yourself and complete the work within this book. I've referenced this before, but I use Danielle LaPorte's Weekly Planner as a companion to my journal. In it, she has "soul prompts," a daily reminder of how you have the power to choose how you want to feel every day.

Other Resources and Tools

Podcasts/TED talks: If, like me, you enjoy the process of learning new ideas or concepts, or you simply want to feed your mind with a new perspective that helps you in your personal growth, I recommend and love podcasts and/or TED talks for this purpose. You can search for podcasts by subject in the podcast app and listen on your commute, while you exercise, or while you clean, for example. There is also a TED talk app, and you can search by topic there as well. The goal here is to feed your mind with positivity and inspiration while you work through your emotional challenges. I often listen to positive affirmation podcasts (Louise Hay being one of them) while I mow the lawn. I'm all about making the mundane tasks of life fun or a learning experience. I encourage you to try it, as it does make the task at hand less mundane.

• **Exercise:** Possibly my least favorite activity mentioned thus far but, in my opinion, one of the most important. Chemically, things happen within our bodies when we exercise. No one can dispute the positive influence exercise has on our brains. But, just as working through emotional trauma is painful, so is exercise—at first. Which explains why so many avoid it because how can pain possibly equal pleasure? It's the gains, the payoff in the end, that gets to the core of your reason for wanting to exercise before you even start. Once you have your mission statement for why you want to work out (beyond "I want to lose 10 pounds"), you will be more likely to stick with it. I have struggled with this myself from time to time. I've gone through phases of working out daily to not at all for weeks on end. And I know without a doubt the difference I feel when I don't exercise and when I do. For me, I want to be a positive influence on my children. And I also don't want to be dependent on others to care for me sooner than I have to. I want to be able to enjoy retirement and live long enough to see grandchildren and not be in a wheelchair if I can help it.

The key is finding something you enjoy enough that you will commit to doing it long-term. Of course, you have to listen to your body and consult with a physician before you start any exercise regimen. I think it starts in your mind: changing the story that you tell yourself about exercise. Maybe it doesn't have to be viewed as a regimen. Maybe it could be more about showing your body self-love, making you a priority.

I got a treadmill over a year ago, and it was the best decision I made. I live in a very rural area and we don't have paved roads in my town. This leaves me the options of running on the highway or around town. Come fall and spring, it's a soupy mess of mud to boot. So, I invested in a treadmill I would *enjoy* using. And I think that's key—I like using it. It has certain features that make using it more of a pleasure. And you don't have to run, you can walk. Just walking can be an excellent exercise. Add in some hills or an incline, keep a good pace, and it can be a low-impact anaerobic (which is where you burn fat—bonus!) exercise. You don't have to make it complicated. Enjoy the quiet, letting the walk be your meditation, or add in some great music, an audio book, podcast, or TED talks, and you have yourself a wonderful way to make YOU a priority.

Another key with exercising is having a goal in mind. Maybe you want to get off a particular medication, reduce your cholesterol number, or just overall wake up feeling more energetic. Whatever it is, it can definitely help to write it down and keep it where you can see it. Even better, commit to a 5K or some other event, with or without a partner. Having a partner holds you even more accountable and keeps you from backing out, but paying a registration fee and completing it alone can do wonders.

• **Lastly, surround yourself with others that have the same goal**. Having an accountability group has been tremendous in helping me stick to my goals, no matter what program I'm doing at the time. Often, my friends and I are doing the same workout program. This is great because you also have someone who may share the same struggles. Get a group of friends who share the same wellness goal and decide how often you'll commit to exercise. As a group, choose a program everyone can agree to or meets everyone where they are, and every time you work out, you text "workout done." You don't have to do the same program, but it does make the process more fun, especially in the beginning.

When you have a support system rallying behind you and when you see everyone else has worked out but you, even if it is 8 pm and you're feeling tired, the accountability of having partners may be the very thing that pushes you to get off the couch and make it happen.

I don't believe you need a gym membership to make exercise happen. I think an accountability group offers far more support and success rate than if you were to go to a gym on your own. Unless, that is, you are participating in gym classes where people expect you to show up every week.

Find what works for you and your personality as far as workouts. There are a ton of free resources on the web nowadays that allow you to work out at home with little equipment. Add in accountability partners, and you're well on your way to feeling more energetic, having more confidence, and improving your state of mind.

Some of my favorite workout-from-home resources include: Beach Body Online Membership or programs to purchase, Cody App, YouTube videos (Yoga by Adriene is a personal favorite), SwerkIt App, Sweat by Kayla App, Instagram search, to name a few, and many more. Consult with your physician if you're unsure, experiment, and don't be afraid to mix things up or try something new.

Ongoing Personal Growth

Ongoing growth for me today looks like this: continue reading (non-fiction) books (Brene Brown's books are next on my list) or listen to podcasts or mp3s that teach or inspire me. I also like to watch programs that show me another perspective or that inspire or motivate me (TED talks are perfect for this, and there is a TED app, which can be found on iTunes). I also continue to journal several times a week, exercise regularly, and practice meditation (via the Calm app available on iTunes) and yoga. I feed my mind and body with things that make me feel healthy, productive, and mentally stronger. Before this, it was utilizing programs, books, and my life coach, Angela Goodeve, as well as a lot of writing. And trust me when I say that when I start to neglect to do the things that spiritually, emotionally, and physically nourish me, my physical body reminds me negatively. I believe tension, anxiety, and frustration manifest themselves within our bodies. Keep your well-being on your to-do list—it's so important to your overall health.

That being said, what works for me may not work for you. What I find enjoyable and nourishing to my spirit may not be your cup of tea either. The recipe for success begins with starting; meeting yourself right where you're at. Get real with yourself and look ahead and find a way to gain the momentum needed to start creating progress and change. Once you get going on a path of self-growth, you'll find the things that seemed so frustrating or would once have caused a great emotional upset suddenly roll off your shoulders with a little more ease.

The resources mentioned are a starting point; ideas to get the feelings of necessary change flowing. You may, at some point, find you need outside help. The feelings that rise may be too painful to bear. In that circumstance, be kind to yourself. It's not a sign of weakness. I believe it takes more courage to ask for help than to hide from that which torments the soul.

Conclusion

"In the broken places, the light shines through."

- Leonard Cohen

Just like life, we go through stages of growth. The need to grow may be sparked by one traumatic experience, a series of events stacked one after another, or a mid-life crisis. If we never deal with the hand that's been dealt to us in life, we carry it into our future. We end up changing ourselves to match our surroundings, or we try to change everyone else. Neither serves us or ends well.

My hope is this: that reading my story inspires you to take stock of where you've been, how it's changed you (both positive and negative), where you want to go, what you want to achieve, and motives you to map a plan on what you need to do to achieve it. It is never too late to start. It is never too late to mend broken fences (just as I did after thirty years). It is never too late to heal your heart, shift your mindset, and change your life. If not today—*when?*

Trust me when I say this: you can choose to have a more positive impact on the world around you, or you can let your circumstances dictate your future and be the negative influence towards everything you bring into your life. You do have a choice—*always*. Own that responsibility; make this one life you've been given the very best it can be. Let the very best of you out for the world to see. It's like the saying goes, "Smile and the world smiles back at you."

I've shared the grief in my life as a way to express that, even under difficult beginnings, the narrative can be changed. I am no one special. I'm a girl from a small town, with a difficult childhood, who realized, to give to the world in a meaningful way, I had to shift my thinking from being a victim to recognizing the strength and the wisdom gained in my circumstances. There is nothing special about me, because I believe you can create this change in your life as well. You, too, can change your narrative and forever let go of the emotional ties that keep you bound to your past.

What people don't talk about is how grief never goes away. To say it does would be to say that our love, too, goes away. It's natural to feel a shadow of that grief in quiet moments of remembrance, when life itself inspires a thought within us that brings us back to our grief. Just the mere fact that our daily pattern is different is, in itself, a reminder. Shift the narrative the moment those times arrive. Pause and recognize those thoughts, allowing them to pass through, accepting that death is a process of life and we can't escape it. However, understand we can choose to live our own life to the fullest while we still have the opportunity.

Speaking of opportunity, I took advantage of it when I learned of my uncle's illness. I previously mentioned, my faith led me to reach out to my uncle when I learned he was in the hospital. And, just last week, as I began the editing phase of this book, he passed away. There were several more visits after the initial one and will forever cherish the time we did have together. Suffice to say, I am filled with heavy sorrow for the lost time I could have spent sharing my life with his, getting to know him, and hearing all the stories of my dad I had never before heard. So, I grieve all over again. And I know I will again in the future. It is the one certainty I have. The difference between today and years ago, however, is my mind is in a very different place. And it would seem that everything happens in the right time, space, and sequence, even if it is painful. What I have now, from those visits, is a reconnection of my past and a rekindling of relationships I thought were long lost.

When you have experienced grief (or other forms of emotional trauma), it will, understandably, shake your foundation, regardless of your age. What I wish to discover, though, is how differently it affects us depending on when we experience grief or emotional trauma. I wonder, do those who don't experience grief/emotional trauma until well into adulthood react differently and have a more difficult time moving on than those who've had an experience such as my own? Perhaps this is an idea to explore for a future book. Because, I sometimes wonder how I got to where I am today. How did I overcome my emotional pain and not end up on a very different path in life? I have asked myself this question many times over the years.

For me, I conclude it all started with prayer. And at the time, in my early twenties, I was not the praying type. My struggles brought me to God. Isn't that what God wants for us? To be drawn *to* him? Then my husband, only a friend for several years, re-emerged in my life in a way I never imagined. It's as if a switch went off in his mind and suddenly he wanted a relationship—*with me?* To this day, I can ask my husband what made him suddenly decide to pursue me, and I don't get a straight answer—as if he doesn't really know. But he (with the help of God) saved me from myself.

What I'm telling you, though, is despite my renewed faith, my ability to let go of past pain was a several-decades-long journey. It took motherhood, entrepreneurship, and more grief to decide that working on myself was the best investment I could ever make for myself and for my children. And, as soon as I started to do that, I felt more confident as a parent, new ideas and visions began to emerge for what I wanted my future to look like, and real changes began to occur within.

Do I think you have to find spirituality and faith to move past grief and emotional pain? I certainly believe so now. In my early twenties, I wouldn't have heard any of this. I would have thought it was all a little "woo woo." Maybe you do, too, which is entirely understandable—especially if this is the first book on grief you're reading. Because it's almost taboo to talk about death and dying, isn't it? We ignore it until there's a funeral, where we're reminded of our own mortality. And maybe that's the difference then? That I've been reminded every day of my life since I was eight? It just took me a lot longer to process that fact—maybe because of my age when I experienced it? Maybe because of other emotional traumas that stacked on top of it? I don't know.

What I do know is that faith is the foundation of my life today. Without it, I wouldn't be writing this book. Without faith, I wouldn't have taken a chance on so many great adventures I've had in my life. I also wouldn't have felt that everything that happens in my life is for my greater good— even if I don't understand it at the time. Having faith and being able to let go of what was yesterday or thirty years ago has liberated me of a lot of emotional baggage.

When we remove the mental clutter (which for me is a daily practice that isn't easy by any means), we allow new ideas or inspired thought to flow through us. But first, it takes a leap of faith: trusting the process of self-discovery and resisting the urge to resist. When feelings start bubbling to the surface that make you uncomfortable, it's easy to let fear get in the way. And like a tortoise that ducks back into its shell when it senses danger, you'll have the same knee-jerk reaction. Resist the urge to bypass that which can help you grow. That is my message: whatever the self-discovery journey looks like for you, stick with it.

I believe wholeheartedly (because I didn't have it during the most important years of my life) that having faith and spirituality as a part of your life makes the journey of self-discovery less painful. I think there is much in this life we will never understand and the only thing we can actually learn to understand is ourselves.

When we hold the mirror to ourselves and really look within, it's scary at first. Having a foundation to come back to, however, even during the most difficult of realizations, will help you stick with it. It's having faith that there is something better to come, despite all the pain of the past.

I'm reminded of a message I heard while watching an interview with Elizabeth Vargas on the ABC show, *20/20*, regarding her personal story with alcohol addiction. She said, "When you pray to God, you get one of three answers: *yes, not now, or I have something better for you.*" I couldn't agree more.

I've shared the most vulnerable parts of myself. I encourage you to do the same. I don't believe there's any other way to heal than to allow yourself the time and the space to be vulnerable. I've given you examples and resources to help you get started, but also know you can reach out to me. Go to my website, www.theguidedheart.com, and there you will find a contact page. Likewise, you can reach out to me on my Facebook page at Facebook.com/TheGuidedHeart for those currently grieving or who are struggling to get out of their grief. If my story resonates with you, I encourage you to reach out and share yours. There's healing in acknowledgment.

Work on getting mentally and spiritually strong and there isn't anything life can throw at you that will bring you down. I don't believe we have to experience emotional trauma to grow. However, I do believe, for those that do, it is a gift. When we do our best to learn from every situation handed to us, and we become a student of life, only then can we become the teacher, guiding and holding the hands of others, saying, "I've been there too."

Consider this book an expression of my love and compassion for your struggle, and my way of holding your hand and saying, "You're not alone."

"Peace I leave with you, my peace I give to you: not as the world gives, give I to you. Let not your heart be troubled, neither let it be afraid."

- John 14:27

Gratitude

*"Thank You for making me so wonderfully complex!
Your workmanship is marvelous - and how well I
know it."*

- Psalm 139:14 (NLT)

My Lord, creator of heaven, earth, and every cell of my very being and soul, I give thanks for this life I've been given. Albeit at times taking it for granted and wishing to be a bird, so I could fly far, far, far away from here, like the young Jenny Curran character stated in the movie *Forrest Gump*. I find my strength through you, Lord. You keep me grounded and draw me towards you in times of weakness.

My dad. The root of my deepest sorrow and the mountain of my greatest triumph. I've finally found purpose to your life and to your death. I am grateful for the lessons your soul has brought me and I pray I can be a beacon of light for other grieving hearts. I also pray I see you again one day. In the meantime, I feel your spirit—now more than ever.

My love, Tony—the rock and foundation of our family. Your willingness to oversee my shortcomings and encourage the best parts of me has helped me bloom where I'm planted. You understand me better than I do myself at times and always know exactly what I need without me having to say a word. I love you.

My little loves: Xavier, Alexandra, and Jozlyn. You have brought the full spectrum of emotion into my life, at times on a daily basis. Through each of you, I have found a love that can't compare to any other, I have learned patience, and I see the world differently because of each of you. Thank you for bringing your wisdom, sunshine, and spunk into my life each and every day.

My mom, sister, brother, and brother and sister through marriage: each of you have influenced my life and shaped me into the person I am today. You've seen me at my best and also my worst. I am grateful for forever knowing I have your support and love.

My dear friends: you know who you are. To know you'll pick up when I call, trusting you will forever stand beside me, and feeling accepted for who I am—quirks and all—is the greatest gift you have given me.

My life coach and friend, Angela Goodeve. You helped me climb out of a deep pit. Your wisdom and compassion got me from week to week. I adore your beautiful soul and Canadian accent. I pray one day we meet so I can give you the most grateful hug. You greatly influenced this book— more than words can say. Namaste!

Roger and family. You opened your hearts to the past and welcomed my presence. Your openness was instrumental in healing my broken heart of the past. I am grateful for the few months we shared, Roger, and although it was brief, the experience of bringing you (and your family) into my life has changed mine for the better.

My book-writing coach, Kathy Wheeler. Without you, this book that's been on my heart for a couple years may have never seen the light of day. I am grateful you created your program, for the friend who just so happened to know you, and for the perfect timing of it all; a sign to me that there were angels at work in my life. This is a very different book now than it would have been years past. For your guidance and patience, I am forever grateful.

My editor, Emily Nemchick. You were a perfect match and I am so grateful for you sharing your skills with the world and with me. You have a way of making this "wordy gal" a lot less "wordy." You went above and beyond and any future book I write will definitely require your finishing touch.

My dear reader. I pray this book brings you solace and hope, if you're a grieving heart. If you know someone grieving, my hope is this book brings you understanding. If you're struggling right now, there is always help and there is hope; you just have to dig a little deep. Feel it. All of it. So you, too, can let it go.

"If everyone were to bring their miseries together in one place, most would be glad to take their own home again rather than take a portion out of the common stock."

- SOLON (638-558 B.C.)

About the Author

Having experienced multiple traumatic events in her childhood, including the death of her father to cancer at age 8, Victoria had to grow up fast. The author takes you by the hand and along with her on her personal growth story, all the while weaving in her experience with childhood grief. The message she shares is one of hope that, despite grief never leaving, it can make you stronger emotionally and spiritually.

Victoria, an entrepreneur and creative at heart, has been writing in blog form since 2009 and has had her writing featured on TheMogulMom.com. She is a committed student of life, continually looking for ways to grow and understand the world around her. She resides in rural ND with her husband and three children. She enjoys hearing others stories of grief and triumph and encourages you, the reader, to reach out via email or, if you prefer snail mail, put your soulful words to paper and mail your letter directly. Receiving non-bill mail would bring Victoria great joy and you positive karma.

Victoria Volk
P.O. Box 64
Hague, ND 58542

Victoria can be found at: www.theguidedheart.com,
@victorialvolk on Instagram, or at
www.Facebook.com/TheGuidedHeart

For inquiries, email directly at:
victoria@theguidedheart.com

www.ingramcontent.com/pod-product-compliance
Lightning Source LLC
LaVergne TN
LVHW051102080426
835508LV00019B/2019